Wild Game Chilies, Soups, and Stews

Rick Black

STACKPOLE BOOKS

0 11557 03277 2

To my grandson Gavin for being Grandpa's boy. Just like your pop,
you will spend many hours hunting, fishing, and camping with me,
and all the outdoor fun in between. Already Grandpa's grills and
Dutch ovens fascinate you.

Copyright © 2008 by Stackpole Books

Published by

STACKPOLE BOOKS
5067 Ritter Road
Mechanicsburg, PA 17055
www.stackpolebooks.com

Printed in the United States

First edition

10 9 8 7 6 5 4 3 2 1

Cover design by Wendy A. Reynolds

Illustrations by Daniel Roberts

Library of Congress Cataloging-in-Publication Data
Black, Rick.
  Wild game chilies, soups, and stews / Rick Black. — 1st ed.
      p. cm.
  Includes index.
  ISBN-13: 978-0-8117-3277-2 (alk. paper)
  ISBN-10: 0-8117-3277-0 (alk. paper)
  1. Cookery (Game) I. Title.
TX751.B57 2007
641.6'91—dc22

                                                              2007020606

CONTENTS

ACKNOWLEDGMENTS

My thanks for help in furnishing data, photos, and for sharing time, knowledge, and experience go to Chef Peter Harman (The Food Guru) for his great teaching and coaching; Cosmo of The New Mix 107.3 Morning Show; Terry Lee for his outstanding computer support; Dan Roberts (my cartoon master) for his great work on my outdoor columns and books, including this one; Brad Holland of Holland Grill, Camp Chef (Cousin Rick's way to the outdoors); Steve Daugherty, Jim Kannenberg, and Kathy Anderson of Quarry Creek Elk & Bison for their outstanding support and great-tasting elk and buffalo meat; Tim and the gang of Fleck Sales (Miller and Miller Lite) beer men; John Dunnegan from 101.7 The Bull; Jim Ferguson from the Great American Outdoor Trails radio magazine; Robin Delaney from the *Fort Madison Daily Democrat*; Gamo Precision Airguns; Sparky Sparkes from M2d Camo; Ted Nugent; Coach/Chef Jeff Schuster; and Baja Motorsports.

INTRODUCTION

The successes of my previous wild game books inspired me to write this one on wild game soups and stews. Cooking with wild game has and will always be a passion of mine. I truly enjoy every aspect of it. Many folks say, "I got a freezer full of wild game, and I didn't step one foot into the timber to get it." To those folks I quickly reply, "I'm sorry about your luck!"

My thoughts are there is a difference in how a person cooks and how a meal tastes when you are the hunter who brought those vittles home. The planning, scouting, shot, and the bragging rights are all part of wild game cooking. As I have stated in all my books, great-tasting wild game starts with the field dressing and cleaning of the animal. Always, and I mean always, go the extra mile to have a well-cleaned harvest.

Next, try some of my wild game soup tips and hints. I have found that the best wild game soups are made with a base of homemade stock and fresh ingredients. Obviously this can be a time-consuming endeavor. You can reduce your time in the kitchen by using canned or frozen broths or bouillon bases.

Even so, plan on taking your time with a good soup or stew. Fresh ingredients are best, but some canned or frozen vegetables will work well, such as peas, green beans, and one of my favorites, corn.

A hot soup will help recondition the palate between meal courses or after kicking back a few cold ones. Ideally, cold soups should be served in chilled dishes.

If your soup is not served as the main course, you can count on one quart to serve about four hungry hunters. As a main dish, plan on about two servings per quart.

Since liquids boil at a lower temperature at high altitudes, you might need to extend my recipe cooking times at altitudes above 2,500 feet. Speaking from experience!

To reduce the fat content, make the soup the day before, and then chill and scrape off the fat that rises to the top. If you don't have the time to chill the soup, use an unprinted paper towel to soak up that fat from the surface.

Savory wild game soups and stews always taste better if you make them a day or two in advance and reheat them just before serving. I have been known to cook up a large pot of stew two weeks before leaving Iowa to hunt. Loading up frozen soups and stews is just as common for me anymore as loading up my gear and weapons.

I always check the seasonings of cold soups just before serving. I have found that chilled foods tend to dull the taste buds and will need more seasoning than hot soups and stews.

If your hot soup ends up slightly salty, add a whole, peeled potato to the soup and simmer for about 20 minutes to absorb the salt. Remove the potato and serve. (Make sure to save the tater fer yourself—good eatin'.)

Be aware that herbs will have more intense flavor if added at the end of the long cooking process. I think wine is a great flavor addition to soups and stews. When using wine or alcohol in soup, use less salt, as the wine tends to intensify saltiness. Wine should be added at a ratio of no more than $1/4$ cup of wine to 1 quart of soup or stew.

Beer is a great addition to soups and stews! Your old Cousin Rick loves cooking with beer. In fact of the many cookbooks I have written, *Cooking with Beer* is still one of my most popular amongst hunters and city folks. A good rule of thumb is 1 cup beer to 3 cups of soup.

Whether you're having warm weather or cold weather right now, there is a wild game soup just perfect for your climate. A steaming bowl of hearty wild game soup can warm you to your toes at deer camp.

One factor hunters face when cooking wild game soup is how to thicken it. I think the best method to thicken most soups and stews is to remove some of the cooked vegetables, puree in a blender, and return the pureed mixture to the pot. If you are short on veggies or there are none in your soup, make a paste of flour mixed with twice as much cold stock, milk, or water. Add the paste and stir slowly at a simmer for about 10 minutes. I use a ratio of $1^1/_2$ teaspoons of flour to 1 cup of soup. A roux of butter and flour can also be used as a thickener. The longer the roux is cooked, the darker and more flavorful it becomes. Cream is another alternative to not only thicken but also add a luxurious richness. A cornstarch slurry of 1 part cornstarch to 2 parts liquid will also thicken, but should not be boiled because it will break down.

So how about a little history on soups and stews (something to tell the boys at camp while you're cookin')? Food historians say that the history of soup is probably as old as the history of cooking. Considering almost all meat back then was harvested by packs of early-day hunters, wild game soups and stews are part of hunting history. The word *soup* most likely came from the Latin verb *suppare,* soak, which was said to be borrowed from the German root *(sup-)* as in sup and supper. This meant a meat broth poured into or over bread. Cool, ain't it! Who said that being a Cousin Rick fan meant you was a hick. . . .

As in all wild game, all hunters must always follow a few commonsense rules before cooking their wild game harvest.

PROPER FOOD SAFETY

Thoroughly cooking wild game meat is important to reduce the likelihood of any bacterial disease. All wild game meat should be cooked until the meat is no longer pink and the juices run clear. Here are a few more tips for safe handling of wild game:

- Hunters should not handle or consume wild animals that appear sick or act abnormally, regardless of the cause.
- Always wear heavy rubber or latex gloves when field-dressing wild game.
- If the intestinal contents contact meat, consider the meat contaminated; cut off and discard the affected area.
- Handle carcasses properly. Cool the carcass rapidly in the field. (Bags of ice or snow can hasten cooling.) Age the carcass at or below 40 degrees for no longer than 5 to 7 days.

Hang birds by feet at below 40 degrees for 2 to 3 days maximum.

- Hold meat at or below 40 degrees at all times. If you don't plan to consume or process the meat within 3 to 5 days, freeze it. Thaw frozen meat only in the refrigerator, *never* at room temperature.
- Wash your hands with soap and water before and after handling wild game meat.
- Sanitize your equipment and work surfaces often during handling and processing meat and poultry; use a bleach solution of 1 tablespoon bleach to 1 gallon of water.
- Use a meat thermometer to cook meat to proper temperatures. There are several types of meat thermometers available, which are easy to use and can be read instantly or remain in meat while it cooks. This helps ensure that harmful bacteria are killed and the meat is not overcooked. The color of meat is an unreliable indicator of doneness. At the very least, always cook until no longer pink and the juices run clear.

In this book I will share with you some of my favorite wild game and seafood soup and stew recipes. Hoping to write the most complete wild game soups and stews cookbook that any hunter will cherish for years to come, I cover small game, big game, game birds, seafood, and exotics.

I start with wild game chili and then small game (rabbit, squirrel, beaver, muskrat, opossum, raccoon, armadillo, and others). I then tackle big game (whitetail, antelope, boar, buffalo, bear, caribou, elk, moose, wild goat, wild sheep, and a few other critters). The game bird chapter includes great-tasting recipes for grouse, partridge, squab, quail, pheasant, wild duck, wild geese, and wild turkey, just to name a few. The seafood chapter has it all, from crab to salmon, with a few other critters that make bubbles under the water in between.

Wild game and soup go together like a guitar and Ted Nugent. So grab your deer burger from the freezer, and let's get ready for some country boy cookin'!

CHAPTER ONE

WILD GAME CHILI

Without a doubt chili is the most common soup made by hunters. And why not? Cookin' wild game chili is a blast! There are so many flavors you'd be dizzier than a wood tick if you tried them all. That's where your old Cousin Rick comes in! I have tossed the cabin sink in this chapter! I love chili. The way I see it, chili, like apple pie, is an American icon. And although you may think it is Mexican, it isn't. Chili as we know it is not served in Mexico, except for areas that cater to tourists. Now there's something to chat about.

There are many tales out there on the twists and turns in the history of chili. For example, one story is that chili was invented by chuck wagon cooks who traveled along with cowboys on long cattle drives across the rugged hills and deserts of the great Southwest. I was told that, as they traveled in one direction, the cooks planted oregano, chiles, and onions among patches of mesquite to give them protection from the hot sun, foraging cattle, and other critters. Then on their way back along the same trail, they would collect the spices, combine them with chopped venison or beef and call it Trail Drive Chili.

A few years ago I was deer hunting in Missouri with a few good old boys who told me that chili was an invention of the Texas prison systems in the early times because the prisons bought the cheapest and toughest cut of meat. To make them more palatable, they took cleavers and knives to the meat to create little pieces that were then boiled, along with chiles and spices, to create a cheap and satisfying meal for the outlaws.

In any case wild game has played a big part in many of chilies cooked up on and off the trails. Take the time and study each and every wonderful chili recipe, and don't let the ingredients scare ya— they are all good!

But first a few chili cooking tips using wild game.

Cooling off: If you made your chili too hot, use ice-cold milk for immediate relief. No matter what Bubba and the boys say, drinking a cold beer goes great with chili; however, it won't stop a mouth of fire!

Using dried chiles versus chile powder: Some recipes in this book call for preparing dried chiles such as ancho or New Mexico varieties. You can substitute a chile powder. One tablespoon of powder per pound of wild game meat is a good place to start. Add half of the total amount of powder initially, gradually adding more to taste. Thus you will read the following after most of my recipes: "Check for seasoning and serve."

Chile powder is not the same as chili powder: The former is pure powdered chiles, while the latter is chile powder and a bunch of other spices (i.e., "instant chili").

Preparing dried peppers: Most peppers can be rehydrated by removing the stems and seeds and soaking or cooking them in hot water. The New Mexico and Anaheim varieties have smooth, tough skin. Do not try the soak-and-blend technique. Instead, cut off the tops of the peppers to remove the stems and seeds and expose the interior. Steep them for an hour in hot water; then cut the peppers in half lengthwise. For each half, carefully scrape off the inner pulp with a flat knife into a blender.

Seasonings: Use salt, black pepper, and bay leaves according to your own taste.

Tasty vittles: When cooking chili with wild game meat, I like to use chicken stock to improve the flavor. Try it, you'll like it!

Thickening: If you want your chili thicker, I recommend you mix a tablespoon of flour with about 3 tablespoons water and stir into the chili for the last 20 minutes of simmering. Many recipes in this chapter will also use masa with cornstarch. The choice is yours.

Bubba's Tons of Beans Chili

$1/4$ pound dried kidney beans
$1/4$ pound dried white beans
$1/4$ pound dried pink beans
$1/4$ pound dried black beans
$1/4$ pound dried red beans
$1/4$ pound dried pinto beans
$1/4$ pound dried cranberry beans
$1/4$ pound dried navy beans
1 pound bacon
5 onions, peeled and chopped
$2/3$ cup minced garlic
$1/4$ cup toasted coriander seeds, ground
$1/4$ cup ground cinnamon
$1/4$ cup paprika
$1/4$ cup cayenne pepper
$1/2$ cup ground dried Poblano chile peppers
108 ounces canned Italian plum tomatoes, with juice
12 ounces beer
5 pounds deer burger

In a large pot, soak the beans together overnight in water to cover. Drain and add fresh water to cover. Cook at a simmer for about 2 hours or until the beans are tender. While the beans are cooking, heat a large skillet. Mince the bacon and cook it until it begins to crisp. Add the onions and garlic, and cook over medium heat for about 5 minutes. Add all the spices and the ground Poblanos, and cook for another 5 minutes. Add the tomatoes with the juice and the beer. Simmer for 30 minutes.

In another pan, cook the deer burger until it is no longer pink. Drain and add it to the tomato mixture. When the beans are fully cooked, drain them, reserving the liquid to add later if necessary, and add the beans to the meat and tomato mixture. Salt to taste and let the soup simmer on low for about 60 minutes. If the soup is too thick, you may add more beer. Check the chili for seasoning and serve.

Cashew Duck Chili

4 yellow onions
2 bell peppers
2 stalks celery
3 cloves garlic
1 teaspoon basil
1 teaspoon oregano
1 tablespoon chili powder
1 teaspoon cumin
32 ounces canned tomatoes
1 bay leaf
1 cup cashews
1 teaspoon salt
$^1/_4$ cup raisins
1 pound cooked duck meat, cubed
3 cups kidney beans
$^1/_4$ cup cider vinegar

Sauté the onions, bell peppers, celery, and garlic. Add the spices and fry with the onion mixture, stirring constantly. Add the tomatoes, bay leaf, cashews, salt, raisins, and duck meat. Add the beans and simmer covered for about 30 minutes. Add the cider vinegar and check for seasoning. Simmer on low for another 20 minutes and serve hot.

Shotgun Chili

1 pound ground rabbit meat, browned
1 diced white onion
1 diced green bell pepper
1 cup diced canned tomatoes
1 cup canned chili beans (hot)
10 ounces tomato paste
$^1/_2$ cup red wine
1 package chili seasoning mix
1 tablespoon chili powder
Sour cream

Mix all the ingredients together and place in a large crock. Cook on low heat for about 8 hours. Check for seasoning and serve hot with a tablespoon of sour cream on top.

Montana Pride Chili

I large chopped onion
12 large jalapeño peppers
6 garlic cloves
2 pounds ground elk meat
I 15-ounce can kidney beans
I 15-ounce can black turtle beans
I 8-ounce can tomato sauce
I tablespoon paprika
I tablespoon cumin
I tablespoon garlic powder
I tablespoon oregano
I teaspoon cayenne
$^1/_2$ teaspoon fresh ground black pepper

Chop the onions, peppers, and garlic. Sauté them in olive oil until the onions are brown and tender. Toss in the ground elk meat and continue cooking until the meat is browned. When the elk is finished cooking, place the meat mixture and all the remaining ingredients into a large crock or stewing pot. If using a slow cooker, cook for about 8 hours on low setting. If using a stew pot, cook covered for about 90 minutes. If more liquid is needed, add beer. Check for seasoning and serve hot.

Snow Top Timber Chili

3 cups soaked red beans
I bay leaf
4 teaspoons cumin
4 teaspoons oregano
4 teaspoons paprika
¹/₂ teaspoons cayenne
I teaspoon chili powder
¹/₂ of I chile negro, or to taste
2 pounds ground elk, browned
Peanut oil
2 chopped onions
5 minced garlic cloves
Salt
4 cups chopped tomatoes, with juice
2 teaspoons chopped chipotle chile
¹/₄ cup red wine
2 tablespoons cider vinegar

Cover the beans and bay leaf with 2 inches of fresh water and bring to a boil in a large pot. Lower the heat and simmer. Toast the cumin and oregano over medium heat, stirring so they don't burn. When they are fragrant, add the paprika, cayenne, and chili powders; toast them for just a few seconds. Remove from heat. Grind with mortar and pestle. Dry the chile negro in a 400-degree oven for about 2 minutes or so. Cool and remove the stem, seeds, and veins. Shred it and then grind in a food processor. Sauté the onion in oil until tender; add garlic, salt, ground herbs, and chile, and cook for about 5 minutes. Add the tomato, juice, 1 teaspoon chipotle, and red wine; simmer for another 20 minutes. Add the beans and more water to cover the beans by about an inch. Cook until the beans are soft (about 60 minutes). Add the browned elk meat and remaining ingredients and simmer for another 60 minutes, checking for seasonings. Serve hot.

Jeff May's Iowa Deer Camp Chili

2 cups dried pinto beans
1 cup dried black beans
2 pounds venison meat, cubed
4 chipotle peppers
1 large yellow onion
$1/4$ teaspoon oregano
$1/3$ cup chili powder
1 tablespoon cumin
6 cloves garlic
2 cups hot salsa

Soak the beans for at least 12 hours. Brown the venison, and drain off any fat. If the chipotles are dried, soak them for about 5 minutes in hot water; then pulverize them with the onion and garlic in a food processor. Add onion, oregano, chili powder, cumin, garlic, venison, and beans to a large slow cooker, with enough water to make soup base. Let the soup simmer for about 12 hours. About 1 hour before serving, add the salsa. Check for seasoning and serve.

Cousin Bob York's Carolina Chili Vittles

1 pound ground bear meat
1 diced green bell pepper
1 large diced onion
1 small can tomato paste
3 15-ounce cans tomato sauce
1 large can stewed tomatoes
3 diced jalapeño peppers
2 teaspoons chili powder
$1/4$ teaspoon cayenne pepper
1 large can kidney beans

Brown the ground bear meat, peppers, and onion. Drain off any fat. Add the remaining ingredients and bring to a boil. Reduce the heat to a low simmer. Cook the bear chili for about 60 minutes. Check for seasonings and serve. Great with cornbread.

Hartschuh's Timber Ghost Chili

1 quart beef broth
2 pounds deer burger
$^1/_4$ cup onion flakes
4 tablespoons chili powder
1 teaspoon ground cumin
$^3/_4$ teaspoon instant minced onions
$^1/_2$ teaspoon salt
$^1/_4$ teaspoon ground allspice
$^1/_4$ teaspoon ground cloves
$^1/_4$ teaspoon cayenne
1 bay leaf
1 15-ounce can tomato sauce
2 tablespoons white vinegar
$^1/_2$ ounce unsweetened chocolate

Boil the beef broth in a large saucepan. Slowly add the deer burger to broth until the meat separates into small pieces. Cover and simmer for about 40 minutes. Add the remaining ingredients and mix well. Bring to a boil; reduce the heat and simmer, covered, for about 60 minutes. Refrigerate overnight. Skim off the fat that is on top; then reheat, check for seasoning, and serve.

Cocky Field Chili

This chili is pure outdoorsmen's bliss.

3 large pheasant breasts
1 1/2 quarts water
1/4 cup finely chopped celery
7 cups peeled, chopped tomatoes
2 teaspoons sugar
6 long green chiles
1 teaspoon oregano
1 tablespoon ground cumin
1/2 teaspoon MSG
1 tablespoon black pepper
4 teaspoons garlic salt with parsley
5 tablespoons chili powder
1 teaspoon cilantro
1 teaspoon thyme
1 cup dark beer
2 garlic cloves, finely chopped
1/2 pound beef suet
5 pounds boar chops, sliced thin
4 pounds elk steak
3 onions, cut in 1/2-inch pieces
3 green peppers, cut in 3/8-inch pieces
1 pound Jack cheese, shredded
Juice of 1 lime

Cut the pheasant breasts into chunks and combine with water in a large pot or kettle. Simmer for about 2 hours and then strain off the broth.

In a 2-quart saucepan combine the celery, tomatoes, and sugar, and simmer for 1 hour. Boil the chiles for about 15 minutes, or until they are tender; remove the seeds and cut them in 1/4-inch pieces. Mix the oregano, cumin, MSG, pepper, garlic salt, chili powder, cilantro, and thyme with beer until all the lumps are dissolved. Add the tomato mixture, chiles, beer mixture, and garlic to the pheasant stock. Melt suet to make about 8 tablespoons of drippings. Pour 1/3 of the suet drippings into the skillet, add 1/2 the boar chops, and brown. Repeat for the remaining boar chops. Add the cooked boar meat to the broth mixture and simmer on low heat for about 30 minutes. Trim all fat from the elk steaks and cut them into cubes. Brown the elk meat in the remaining drippings. Add the cooked elk meat to the wild-boar mixture. Return to a simmer and cook on low heat for about 60 minutes. Add the onions and green peppers; simmer on low heat for 3 hours, stirring with a wooden spoon every 20 minutes or more. Let the soup cool for 1 hour and place it in the refrigerator for 24 hours. Reheat the soup to the desired temperature. Add the cheese 5 minutes before serving. Add the lime juice and check for seasoning.

You're a Cousin Rick Huntin' Hick If:
- Your kid's bike has a gun rack on it.
- You have scars on the back of your hand where Uncle Bubba stabbed you while you were reaching for the last bowl of squirrel chili.
- You can talk for more than 20 minutes on the difference between muskrat and beaver stew.
- Your momma can back down a biker.
- Dressing up is wearing the flannel shirt without any rips in it.
- Your trolling motor used to be a fan in a Laundromat.
- You list tick removal as a skill on your resume.
- The photo on your driver's license includes your coon dog.

Geronimo's Last Stand Chili

2 cups water
$^1/_2$ cup dried pinto beans, soaked overnight and then drained
I tablespoon bacon drippings
I sliced onion
$^1/_2$ green bell pepper, cored, seeded, and chopped
I minced garlic clove
I pound wild-boar meat, cut into $^1/_2$-inch cubes
$^1/_2$ pound elk stew meat, cut into $^1/_2$-inch cubes
16 ounces canned whole tomatoes, drained
2 tablespoons chili powder
I diced green chile
I teaspoon dried oregano
2 teaspoons cumin
$^1/_3$ cup dry red wine
Salt and pepper to taste
2 tablespoons prepared tortilla flour, mixed with water to form a paste

Combine the water and beans in a medium saucepan and bring to boil over medium high heat. Reduce the heat and simmer until tender, about 60 minutes. Heat the bacon drippings in a large skillet. Add the onion, green pepper, and garlic. Sauté until all is tender. Transfer to a Dutch oven and set aside. Add the boar and elk meat to the skillet and brown well. Stir into vegetables in Dutch oven. Add the beans and their liquid along with the tomatoes and seasonings. Mix well, cover, and simmer for about 60 minutes. Add the wine and cook, uncovered, for another 30 minutes or so. Season with salt and pepper. If the mixture is too thin, stir in some of the tortilla flour paste to thicken.

YEP, I'M FROM IOWA

Last fall a truckload of huntin' buddies, lookin' for a place to hunt, pulled into a farmer's yard. Cooter, the driver, went up to the farmhouse to ask permission to hunt the farmer's land. The old Iowa farmer said, "Sure, boys, you can get all the deer you want, but would you fellers do me a big favor? That old mule over there is about dang near twenty years old and very sick with the cancer, but I don't have the heart to shoot her. Would you do it for me?"

Cooter said, "Sure," and headed back for the truck. Walking back, however, he decided to pull a trick on his huntin' buddies. He got into the truck and when they asked if the farmer said it was OK, he said, "No, we can't hunt, but I'm going to teach that old cuss a lesson." With that, Cooter rolled down his window, stuck out his gun, and blasted the mule. As he exclaimed, "There, that will teach him!" a second shot rang out from the truck, and Cousin Rick shouted, "Way to go, Cooter, I got the cow!"

Mississippi Catfish Chili

1 cup chopped green bell pepper

2 minced garlic cloves

2 tablespoons butter

1 teaspoon salt

1 pound red kidney beans, canned

1 pound canned tomatoes, undrained

6 ounces tomato paste

2 pounds catfish fillets, chunked

Sauté the green peppers and garlic in butter until tender. Add the salt and mix well. Add the beans and tomatoes. Cover and simmer for about 20 minutes. Add the catfish, cover, and simmer for another 20 minutes, or until the fish flakes easily. Check for seasoning and serve.

Walkers Lake Catfish and Red Bean Chili

2 tablespoons oil
1 large onion, minced
3 garlic cloves, minced
2 tablespoons chili powder
1 teaspoon cumin
$1/2$ teaspoon coriander
1 teaspoon cinnamon
1 teaspoon oregano
$1/2$ teaspoon cayenne
1 pound canned tomatoes, drained
1 green bell pepper, chopped
1 16-ounce can kidney beans, drained
$1/2$ teaspoon garlic salt
Black pepper to taste
1 pound catfish fillets, diced

In a large saucepan over medium heat, sauté the onions, garlic, chili powder, cumin, coriander, cinnamon, oregano, and cayenne in the olive oil. Stir this mixture for about 2 minutes. Add the tomatoes, green peppers, kidney beans, garlic salt, and pepper to taste. Stir this mixture for another 60 seconds. Place the diced catfish fillets on top of the chili mixture and gently stir them into the chili mixture. Simmer on low heat for about 15 minutes and serve.

Jesse Johnson's Gator Chili

The pride of Hamilton, Illinois!

1 pound alligator meat
Garlic salt and pepper to taste
2 tablespoons oil
1 yellow onion, chopped
1 garlic clove, minced
1 red bell pepper, chopped
16 ounces canned pinto beans
10 ounces canned tomatoes with chilies, blended
6 ounces canned tomato paste
1 teaspoon cumin
1 jalapeño pepper, chopped
1 cup dry red wine

Cut the meat into small pieces and remove the tallow. In a Dutch oven, boil the diced meat in water seasoned with garlic salt and pepper for about 25 minutes. Drain and set aside. In the same pot add oil, onion, garlic, and bell pepper. Sauté until the onions are tender. Add the pinto beans, tomatoes, tomato paste, garlic salt, pepper, cumin, and jalapeño. Simmer on low heat for about 3 hours. Add the wine and check for seasoning during the last 30 minutes of cooking.

Stanfield Swamp Alligator Chili Soup

3 pounds alligator meat, diced
¹/₂ cup oil
2 cups diced white onions
I cup diced celery
I cup diced red bell pepper
2 tablespoons diced garlic
2 tablespoons diced jalapeños
I 16-ounce can pinto beans
3 8-ounce cans tomato sauce
I cup chicken stock
I tablespoon chili powder
I teaspoon cumin
Salt and pepper to taste

In a large chili pot, heat oil and add the alligator meat. Cook for about 25 minutes. Add the onions, celery, bell pepper, garlic, and jalapeños. Sauté until the vegetables are tender. Add the pinto beans, tomato sauce, and chicken stock. Bring all to a boil and simmer. Add the chili powder and cumin. Stir well. Simmer for about 60 minutes, stirring every 5 minutes, or until the gator meat is good and tender. Salt and pepper to taste and serve hot.

Destin Shrimp Chili

2 pounds shrimp

4 tablespoons unsalted butter

3 tablespoons olive oil

5 garlic cloves, chopped

2 cups Cousin Rick's BBQ sauce (from my *Grillin' Like a Villain* **cookbook)**

I tablespoon Worcestershire sauce

I teaspoon Louisiana hot sauce

I teaspoon liquid smoke

2 teaspoons red pepper flakes

2 teaspoons sea salt

I teaspoon white pepper

I tablespoon chili powder

1/2 cup chopped parsley

I large lemon, thinly sliced

Peel and clean the shrimp. Melt the butter and olive oil in a large skillet. Add the garlic and sauté until all is tender. Add the shrimp and cook until pink. Add Cousin Rick's BBQ sauce, Worcestershire sauce, hot sauce, liquid smoke, red pepper flakes, sea salt, pepper, and chili powder. Simmer for about 10 minutes. Add the parsley and lemon slices. Simmer for another 8 minutes or so. Check for seasoning and serve hot in soup bowls or over cooked white rice.

Detour Village Black Bear Chili Soup

5 pounds bear roast, chopped into $^1/_4$-inch cubes

5 tablespoons chili powder

2 teaspoons oregano

I teaspoon cayenne

I tablespoon ground cumin

$^1/_2$ pounds smoked bacon

2 tablespoons bacon drippings

I large white onion, chopped

I clove garlic, minced

I red bell pepper, seeded and chopped

12 ounces dark beer

3 cups vegetable juice

14 ounces canned tomatoes and juice

I teaspoon brown sugar

I tablespoon masa harina

Remove all fat from the black bear roast and chop into cubes. Add the chopped meat into a large mixing bowl and sprinkle with chili powder, oregano, cayenne, and cumin. Stir the ingredients well to coat the bear meat. Cover the bowl and chill for 4 hours. Fry up the bacon, drain it on paper towels and cut into pieces, reserving two tablespoons of bacon drippings. In a large pot, heat the bacon drippings, onions, garlic, and red pepper, and cook until all is tender. Add the diced seasoned bear meat to the pot. Cook, stirring often, until the bear meat is browned. Add the beer, vegetable juice, tomatoes, and bacon to the pot. Bring the mixture to a low boil. Add the remaining ingredients and simmer on low heat for about 2 hours. Check for seasoning and serve hot.

BUBBA AND THE GRIZZLY

Bubba was telling his friend about his recent deer-hunting trip to Montana. "We were out in the woods all morning and our guide decided that we should take a break along the riverbank. I wasn't feeling tired so I went for a stroll while the others were resting. As I was walking, a big grizzly bear busted out of the brush in front of me. I turned and started running like heck through the woods with the big bear after me. The bear almost caught up with me but slipped and fell down. I kept running and the bear almost caught up with me again twice, but slipped and fell each time. I finally reached the riverbank.

"The guide saw the bear chasing me and shot it dead."

"Holy smokes!" replied his buddy. "That's incredible. If I were you, I would have soiled myself."

Bubba answered, "What the heck do you think the bear was slipping on?"

Mountain Goat Chili

2 tablespoons vegetable oil

2 cups chopped white onions

1 tablespoon ground oregano

2 tablespoons ground cumin

1 teaspoon garlic powder

1 tablespoon seasoned salt

1 teaspoon cayenne pepper

3 pounds lean ground mountain goat meat

$1/2$ cup plus 2 tablespoons chili powder

$1/2$ cup flour

8 cups boiling water

In a heavy pot, sauté the onions in oil. Add the oregano, cumin, garlic powder, salt, and cayenne pepper. Stir and sauté until the onions are clear. Add the ground mountain goat meat; cook and stir until the meat is crumbly and almost gray. Add the chili powder and then the flour, stirring vigorously until thoroughly blended. Add the boiling water, bring the mixture to a boil, and simmer for about 40 minutes. Check for seasoning and serve.

Fence Row Pheasant Chili

$^1/_2$ cup olive oil

4 pheasant breasts, cubed

2 tablespoons cumin

2 tablespoons chili powder

$^1/_4$ cup chopped garlic

1 red bell pepper, diced

1 yellow bell pepper, diced

1 orange bell pepper, diced

2 large yellow onions, diced

$^1/_2$ cup celery, sliced

2 fresh bay leaves

1$^1/_2$ cups flour

2 quarts chicken broth

1 pint whole whipping cream

4 15-ounce cans cannellini beans

1 15-ounce can kidney beans

3 ancho peppers, diced

Salt and white pepper to taste

Nacho chips and 1 fist full of fresh cilantro

Heat a large stockpot until it is very hot, and then add the olive oil and brown the pheasant meat. Add the cumin and chili powder, cook for about 2 minutes, and then add the garlic. Add the peppers, onion and celery and stir well. Add two fresh bay leaves and the flour, and stir well. Add the chicken broth, cream, and beans and then stir. Add the ancho chile, and simmer for about 50 minutes. Add the salt and pepper to taste. Serve hot garnished with the nacho chips and a pinch of cilantro.

Cosmo's "Rick Bagged His Limit" Pheasant Chili

2 pheasant breasts, chopped
Olive oil
1 12-ounce jar of chicken gravy
24 ounces Northern white beans, undrained
6 drops Frank's Red Hot Sauce
2 tablespoons Dijon mustard
14 ounces chicken stock
1 teaspoon garlic salt
1 teaspoon cumin
1 yellow onion, chopped
$^1/_4$ cup pimento, chopped
1 green bell pepper, chopped
1 tablespoon minced parsley
1 can sweet corn, drained
1 teaspoon chili powder
$^1/_2$ teaspoon cayenne pepper

Brown the pheasant meat in olive oil. Put all the ingredients in a large saucepan. Simmer on low heat until all is hot, stirring every 2 minutes. Simmer for about 2 hours, check for seasoning, and serve.

Ohio Tree Rat (Squirrel) Chili Vittles

3 tablespoons cooking oil
2 onions, chopped
3 pounds squirrel meat, coarsely chopped
2 tablespoons Worcestershire sauce
3 garlic cloves, minced
4 tablespoons hot red chile, ground
2 teaspoons cumin
1 teaspoon dried Mexican oregano
2 teaspoons garlic salt
16 ounces kidney beans, soaked, rinsed, and cooked
16 ounces chili sauce

Heat the oil in a large Dutch oven over medium heat. Stir in the onions and cook until tender. Add the tree rat. Break up any lumps with a wooden fork and cook, stirring often, until the meat is evenly browned. Add the Worcestershire sauce and garlic, and cook for another 5 minutes. Stir in the ground chile, cumin, oregano, and garlic salt. Simmer, uncovered, for another 5 minutes or so. Add the cooked beans and chili sauce, and simmer, uncovered, for about 60 minutes. Check for seasoning and serve hot.

Big Horn Caribou Chili

$1/2$ cup vegetable oil
6 pounds ground caribou meat
2 large white onions, minced
2 garlic cloves, minced
2 tablespoons paprika
12 tablespoons chile pepper, or to taste
2 tablespoons cumin
2 teaspoons Cajun spice mix
2 teaspoons dried oregano
1 teaspoon cinnamon
$1/4$ teaspoon fresh ground black pepper
2 teaspoons seasoned salt
1 cup tomato paste
1 tablespoon honey
2 cups canned tomatoes
2 cups beef stock
2 green bell peppers, diced
$1/2$ cup chopped jalapeño peppers
4 tablespoons Frank's Red Hot Sauce

Heat the oil in a large pot and sauté the caribou meat until all is browned. Drain off the fat and add the onions and garlic. Cook until the veggies are tender and translucent. Add the spices and hot sauce and simmer. Add the tomato paste and honey. Stir the mixture well and then add the tomatoes, beef stock, and diced green bell peppers. Add the jalapeños, stir well, and simmer on low heat for about 4 hours. Check the soup for seasonings and serve hot. Note: You may add beer if needed.

Rusty's Arizona "Snake That Rattles" Chili

$3/4$ cup chopped white onion

3 tablespoons olive oil

3 cups parboiled rattlesnake meat

2 cups cooked tomatoes

2 cups cooked pinto beans

3 teaspoons chili powder

$1/2$ teaspoon hot red pepper flakes

I teaspoon Accent

$1/2$ teaspoon white pepper

In a large skillet, sauté the onion in hot olive oil until tender. Add the remaining ingredients. Simmer for about 30 minutes, stirring often. Check the soup for seasoning and add beer if more liquid is needed.

Vinny Moser's Gobbler Chili

3 pounds ground wild turkey

2 cups celery, chopped

6 white onions, finely chopped

2 garlic cloves, minced

2 16-ounce cans diced tomatoes

2 15-ounce cans pinto beans

3 cups spicy vegetable juice

I teaspoon cayenne pepper

I teaspoon cumin

I teaspoon marjoram

3 teaspoons garlic salt

$1/2$ cup chili powder

I tablespoon paprika

2 cups cheddar cheese, shredded

Brown the wild turkey meat in a large pot or soup kettle. Add the celery, onions, garlic, diced tomatoes, and the spicy vegetable juice. Stir well. In a mixing bowl, combine the cayenne, cumin, marjoram, garlic salt, chili powder, and paprika. Sprinkle this mixture over the soup and stir well. Simmer the soup for about 60 minutes, add the beans, stir well, and simmer for another 45 minutes. Check the soup for seasoning, and serve the chili with cheese on top of each bowl.

DECOY

One night during the deer-hunting season a DNR (fish cop) was staking out a well-known rowdy hunting bar for possible DUI violations. At closing time, he saw a deer hunter tumble out of the bar, trip on the curb, and then try his keys in five different trucks before fumbling around with his keys for several minutes. All the other deer hunters left the bar and drove off. Finally the "drunk" started his engine and began to pull away. The fish cop was waiting for him. He stopped the driver, read him his rights, and administered the Breathalyzer test. The results showed a reading of 0. The puzzled officer demanded to know how that could be. The deer hunter replied, "Tonight I'm the designated fish cop decoy."

Meyer's Ranch Turkey Chili Soup

1/2 pound wild turkey breast, chopped

2 cups chopped onions

Oil

3 15-ounce cans Northern white beans

4 cups chicken stock

1 cup beer

1/2 teaspoon onion powder

1/2 teaspoon garlic powder

1/4 teaspoon celery salt

1/2 teaspoon paprika

1/2 teaspoon parsley flakes

1 tablespoon cumin

1/2 teaspoon oregano

2 cups canned white corn

2 chopped green chiles

8 ounces sour cream

Salt and pepper to taste

In a large soup pot or kettle, sauté the turkey with the onions in oil for about 8 minutes, or until the onions are tender. Add the remaining ingredients and stir well. Simmer the chili soup for about 2 hours on very low heat. Check the soup for seasoning and serve hot.

Sergeant Roy's Tough Skin Soup (Armadillo Chili)

3 pounds lean ground armadillo meat
I pound pork sausage
I cup diced white onions
3 chopped garlic cloves
2 cups beer
8 ounces tomato sauce
I cup water
3 tablespoons chili powder
2 tablespoons cumin
2 tablespoons instant beef bouillon
2 teaspoons oregano
2 teaspoons paprika
2 teaspoons sugar
I teaspoon unsweetened cocoa
$^1/_2$ teaspoon ground coriander
I teaspoon Frank's Red Hot Sauce
I teaspoon flour
I teaspoon cornmeal
I tablespoon hot water

In a large Dutch oven, brown half the meat; pour off the fat. Remove the meat and brown the remaining meat; pour off the fat, reserving about 2 tablespoons. Add the onions and garlic; cook and stir until all is tender. Add the cooked meat and the remaining ingredients except the flour, cornmeal, and hot water. Mix well. Bring the soup to a boil; reduce heat and simmer, covered, for about 3 hours. Stir together the flour and cornmeal; add the tablespoon of hot water. Mix well and stir into the chili soup. Cover the soup and simmer for another 30 minutes, stirring often. Check the soup for seasoning and serve.

Hawkeye Muskrat Chili

3 pounds muskrat meat
3 red onions, diced
4 garlic cloves, pressed
I quart whole tomatoes, with juice
4 cups canned kidney beans, with liquid
2 tablespoons chili powder
Salt and pepper to taste

Skin the muskrats and remove all the glands and fat. Parboil the muskrats and onion for about 60 minutes. Remove the meat from the bones and cut into cubes. In a large cast-iron skillet, brown the meat, and add the onions and garlic. Add the remaining ingredients and simmer for 2 hours, uncovered. Check the soup for seasoning and serve hot with crushed Vista Bakery saltines on top. Note: Make it a point to take your time and remove the glands and fat from muskrats. Rat meat is very strong in flavor.

Keokuk Deer Sausage Chili

I tablespoon vegetable oil
I cup chopped yellow onions
I pound ground deer sausage
15 ounces tomato sauce
$^{1}/_{4}$ cup tomato paste
I cup ale
2 tablespoons chili powder
I teaspoon ground cumin
I teaspoon garlic powder with parsley flakes

Heat the oil in a large skillet. Stir in the onions and deer sausage. Cook over medium heat until the onions are tender and the deer sausage is no longer pink. Do not overcook. Drain off the excess fat; add the tomato sauce, tomato paste, beer, chili powder, cumin, and garlic powder. Simmer over medium heat for about 2 hours, stirring often and checking for seasoning.

Cooter's Cabin Buffalo Chili

4 pounds lean buffalo burger
2 large chopped onions
15 ounces tomato sauce
1 tablespoon garlic powder
4 tablespoons chili powder
2 teaspoons cumin
1 teaspoon salt
¹/₂ teaspoon sugar
1 tablespoon Tabasco sauce
4 cups water
2 cups canned black beans, drained

Brown the buffalo meat in small batches. As each batch is finished, transfer to a large stockpot. Add the onions, tomato sauce, garlic powder, chili powder, cumin, salt, sugar, Tabasco sauce, and water. Bring the soup to a boil; reduce the heat to a hard simmer and cook for another 60 minutes. About 30 minutes before the soup is finished cooking, add the drained black beans and simmer for another 30 minutes.

Sullivan Slough Goose Meat Chili

2 cups chopped onions

3 fresh tomatoes, peeled and chopped

3 fresh Anaheims, chopped

2 fresh red bell peppers, chopped

6 carrots, chopped

I tablespoon olive oil

16 ounces dark beer

I teaspoon ginger

4 garlic cloves, minced

2 ounces dried anchos, stems and seeds removed

2 ounces dried pasillas, stems and seeds removed

4 dried japones, stems and seeds removed

I fresh habanero, stems removed

6 cups spicy vegetable juice

3 pounds diced goose breast meat

I teaspoon sage

I teaspoon dill

Place the onion, tomatoes, Anaheims, bell peppers, and carrots in a large soup pot with a tablespoon of olive oil. Cook until tender. Pour the beer into a blender and blend in the ginger and garlic. Add the hot peppers and vegetable juice. Add the goose meat to the pot and brown with the vegetables. Add the blended beer mixture along with the remaining ingredients to the pot and simmer for 4 hours, stirring often. Check the soup for seasoning and serve.

Are You Nuts? Monster Buck Chili

2 tablespoons beef base
48 ounces vegetable juice
1 large onion, diced
1 green bell pepper, diced
1 tablespoon cocoa
5 teaspoons powdered garlic
5 pounds deer burger
6 tablespoons chili powder
1 teaspoon cumin
1 teaspoon black pepper
4 cups butter beans, canned, with liquid

Combine the beef base, vegetable juice, diced vegetables, cocoa, and powdered garlic in a large cooking pot. Simmer on low heat. Divide the deer burger into three equal batches and brown it in a separate skillet. Add the chili powder. When the meat is browned and crumbled, drain the fat and add the cooked deer burger to the pot. Add the remaining ingredients and simmer for 4 hours on low heat.

Feed Your Posse Caribou Chili

Feeds over 30 hungry hunters.

30 pounds ground caribou
3 cups chili powder
I cup brown sugar
$^1/_4$ cup thyme
$^1/_4$ cup salt
$^1/_4$ cup cumin
$^1/_4$ cup garlic powder
12 bay leaves
$^1/_4$ cup oregano
$^1/_4$ cup cayenne
20 quarts tomato juice
12 cups chopped onions
2 quarts peeled tomatoes
30 cups pinto beans

In a very large kettle, brown the caribou with the chili powder. Drain off all fat. Add the remaining ingredients and simmer for 8 hours on low heat. Adjust all seasonings before serving. This is a favorite wild game feed soup. You may add more beans and onions if needed.

Mike Campbell's Body Shop
Grizzly Meat Chili

I cup pinto beans, dried

5 cups water

2 tablespoons lard

I tablespoon bacon drippings

I onion

12 ounces country-style pork sausage

I pound bear meat, chopped

4 garlic cloves

I teaspoon anise

$^1/_2$ teaspoon coriander seeds

$^1/_2$ teaspoon fennel seeds

$^1/_2$ teaspoon ground cloves

I teaspoon cinnamon

I teaspoon black pepper

I teaspoon paprika

I teaspoon ground nutmeg

I teaspoon cumin

2 teaspoons oregano

4 tablespoons sesame seeds

I cup smoked almonds

10 red chiles

2 cups chile caribe

I ounce milk chocolate

I cup tomato paste

2 tablespoons cider vinegar

3 teaspoons lemon juice

Salt to taste

Place the rinsed beans in a bowl, add about 3 cups of water, and soak overnight. Check the beans occasionally and add water as necessary to keep them moist. Pour the beans and water in which they were soaked into a large saucepan and add about 3 more cups of water. Bring the beans and water to a boil; then lower the heat and simmer, partially covered, for about 60 minutes, until the beans are cooked but still firm. Check the beans occasionally and add water if needed. Drain the beans, reserving the cooking liquid. Melt the lard in a large skillet. Add the beans and lightly fry them in the lard. Set the fried beans aside. Melt the bacon drippings in a large pot. Add the onions and cook until tender. Combine the sausage and bear meat with all the spices. Add the spiced meat mixture to the pot with the cooked onions. Break up any lumps of meat with a fork and cook, stirring occasionally, until the bear meat is very well browned. Add the reserved bean cooking water to the pot. Stir in all the remaining ingredients and bring the soup to a low boil. Turn the heat down to a simmer and slowly simmer the soup for about 3 hours. Check the bear chili for seasoning and serve.

WHY HUNTING DOGS ARE BETTER THAN WIVES

- The later you are, the more excited they are to see you.
- Hunting dogs will forgive you for playing with other dogs.
- If a dog is gorgeous, other dogs don't hate it.
- A dog's disposition stays the same all month long.
- Hunting dogs like it if you leave a lot of things on the floor.
- A hunting dog's parents never visit.
- Hunting dogs do not hate their bodies.
- Hunting dogs agree that you have to raise your voice to get your point across.
- Hunting dogs like to do their snooping outside rather than in your wallet or truck.
- Hunting dogs seldom outlive you.
- Hunting dogs can't talk.
- Hunting dogs enjoy petting in public.
- You never have to wait for a hunting dog; they're ready to go 24 hours a day.
- Hunting dogs find you amusing when you're drunk.
- Hunting dogs beg you to go hunting.
- If you bring another dog home, your dog will happily play with both of you.
- A hunting dog will not wake you up at night to ask, "If I died would you get another dog?"
- If your dog has babies, you can put an ad in the paper and sell them.
- On a car trip, your hunting dog never insists on running the heater.

- Hunting dogs don't let magazine articles guide their lives.
- Hunting dogs think Dr. Phil makes about as much sense as you do.
- Hunting dogs love to ride in the back of a pickup truck.
- If a hunting dog leaves, it won't take half your stuff!

Elk Had a "Dumb Attack" Chili Vittles

¹/₄ pound smoked bacon, diced
3 pounds elk stew meat, chili grind
2 pounds wild pig butt, chili grind
2 tablespoons peanut oil
2 cups chopped onions
2 diced jalapeños
2 teaspoons dried Mexican oregano
2 teaspoons ground cumin
2 tablespoons minced serrano
3 tablespoons ground pasilla chiles
2 tablespoons cayenne pepper
2 tablespoons chopped garlic
Salt to taste
2 cups tomato paste
I pound plum tomatoes, diced
8 tablespoons water
2 cups dark beer
I tablespoon lemon juice

Cook the bacon in a skillet over medium heat until crisp, about 5 minutes. Strain and reserve the drippings for another use. Set the cooked bacon aside. Cook the elk meat and wild hog meat in the peanut oil over medium-high heat until brown, about 15 minutes. Add the onions and jalapeños and cook until the onions are tender, about 10 minutes. Add the oregano, cumin, serrano and pasilla chiles, cayenne, garlic, and salt to taste. Stir, and then add the tomato paste, tomatoes, water, and beer. Bring to a rapid boil and then reduce the heat to a simmer. Simmer until the meat is very tender, about 60 minutes. Stir in the reserved bacon and sprinkle with the lemon juice just before serving.

Becky's Moist Beaver Chili

*This recipe don't make Becky happy, but everyone else gets
a kick out of it!*

3 pounds ground beaver chili meat
I cup finely chopped onions
4 garlic cloves, finely chopped
I pound lean ground pork
12 ounces beer
8 ounces tomato sauce
I cup water
4 tablespoons chili powder
2 tablespoons ground cumin
8 beef bouillon cubes
2 teaspoons oregano
2 teaspoons paprika
2 teaspoons sugar
I teaspoon unsweetened cocoa
$^{1}/_{2}$ teaspoon ground coriander
I teaspoon Louisiana hot sauce
I tablespoon flour
I teaspoon cornmeal
I tablespoon hot water

In a large saucepan, brown half of the beaver meat; pour off the
fat. Remove meat; brown the remaining meat; pour off all fat except
2 tablespoons. Add the onion and garlic; cook and stir until the
beaver meat is tender. Add the pork and remaining ingredients
except the flour, cornmeal, and hot water. Mix well. Bring to a boil;
reduce the heat and simmer, covered, for about 2 hours. Stir together the flour and cornmeal; add the hot water and mix it well. Stir
into the chili mixture. Cook covered for another 30 minutes. Check
for seasoning and serve hot.

Minnesota Porcupine Chili Delight

2 pounds porcupine meat, chopped thin
1 large red onion, chopped
3 cloves minced garlic
Butter
3 cups canned stewed tomatoes with juice
5 Anaheim chiles, roasted whole until charred, tossed in a plastic bag
  for about 10 minutes to remove waxy skin, stem, and seeds
2 pickled jalapeños, chopped
6 cups pinto beans
3 cups beef stock
1 teaspoon cumin
$1/4$ teaspoon oregano
1 bay leaf

Cook the porcupine meat in olive oil until most of the moisture is gone; place in a wire screen basket and rinse with hot water until the water seems clear of any fats. Then toss in a large pot. Sauté the onion and garlic in a small chunk of butter until the onion begins to brown, and then toss with the porcupine meat. Add the tomatoes, smashing them with your fingers or cutting them up with kitchen scissors. Add the remaining ingredients, except the beans and a small splash of the liquid from the pickled jalapeños. Bring to a boil and then reduce to a slow simmer for about 60 minutes. Add the beans, check for seasoning and simmer for another 30 minutes. Serve hot.

Old Fort Madison Deer Chili

Serves 100 troopers

30 pounds coarse ground venison

4 pounds chopped onions

2 tablespoons cumin

2 tablespoons oregano

12 ounces chili powder

3 tablespoons salt

3 tablespoons garlic powder

$^1/_4$ cup Tabasco sauce (more or less to taste)

2 pounds mashed tomatoes

5 quarts tomato juice

6 pounds cooked pinto beans, mashed into a paste

Braise the venison meat with the onions in a large pot or kettle. Add the seasonings and stir well. Add the remaining ingredients and simmer for 4 hours, stirring often. Check the soup for seasoning. If you want a thicker soup, add more beans.

Donnellson Quail Chili

4 roasted quails

6 cups water

I pale stalk celery with leaves, coarsely chopped

2 dried cayenne peppers with seeds, split

I teaspoon mustard seeds

I teaspoon dill seeds

I teaspoon white peppercorns

2 cubes chicken bouillon

2 tablespoons butter

I large onion, chopped fine

I minced garlic clove

3 cups chicken stock

I tablespoon fresh basil, chopped

$^1/_4$ teaspoon coriander seeds, crushed

$^1/_4$ teaspoon ground cloves, crushed

4 cups canned great Northern beans, undrained

I tomato, chopped, for garnish

Remove the meat from the roasted quail carcasses and reserve. Boil the quail bones and skin in water seasoned with the celery, dried cayenne peppers (split with seeds), mustard seeds, dill seeds, white peppercorns, and chicken bouillon. Simmer for about 3 hours. Strain out and discard solid matter.

In a Dutch oven, sauté the onion and garlic in butter until tender. Do not brown. Stir in the quail meat pieces and chicken stock. Add the chopped basil. Add the crushed cloves, crushed coriander seeds, and beans with liquid. Heat this mixture to a boil; reduce the heat and simmer, covered, for 60 minutes. Stir often. Check the soup for seasoning and serve with chopped tomatoes as a garnish.

"Mouth on Fire" Rock Cornish Hen Chili (HOT)

2 pounds Cornish hen
2 onions
4 pounds green chiles
I tomato
2 cups tomatillos, canned
I tablespoon oil
2 tablespoons minced garlic
I teaspoon oregano
I teaspoon cumin
2 teaspoons ground red chile
I tablespoon red chile flakes
4 cups chicken broth
3 tablespoons cornstarch

Cut the Cornish hen into ½-inch cubes. Slice the onions lengthwise. Chop chiles, tomato, and tomatillos. Add oil to a heavy skillet, preferably cast iron, and brown meat over high heat. Remove to a large pot or saucepan. Add the onions and garlic to the leftover oil and brown until the onions are tender. Add the oregano, cumin, and red chile, and cook for about 3 minutes. Transfer from skillet to saucepan with Cornish hen meat. Add the tomato, tomatillos, chiles, and chicken stock. Bring to a boil and simmer for about 6 hours. Add water as necessary to maintain the desired consistency. Add the 3 tablespoons of cornstarch mixed with water prior to serving to thicken chili. You may adjust the heat of this chili by adjusting the hot peppers to taste. However, your old Cousin Rick likes it just like this!

Damn That Ram Chili

I large white onion, chopped fine
5 cloves garlic, minced
I teaspoon oregano
I teaspoon cumin
8 fresh long green chiles, roasted, peeled, seeds removed, chopped
I pound wild goat meat, chunked like stew meat
$^1/_4$ cup lime juice
2 cups chicken stock
Salt, pepper, and hot green chiles to taste

In a medium saucepan, sauté the onion, garlic, oregano, and cumin until the onion is clear and tender. Add the green chiles, sauté and stir. Add the wild goat meat and stir to sear all sides of the meat; add lime juice and stir again. Add the chicken stock, stopping when most of the wild goat cubes are covered with liquid. Stir well, reduce the heat to a simmer, cover, and set the timer for about 30 minutes. Check often to make sure nothing is scorching on the bottom. When the timer goes off, check the consistency and add more stock if needed. Add the remaining seasonings and serve hot.

Cousin Rick's Wild Game Chili Feast

Talk about wild game feeds!

100 pounds pinto beans
40 pounds deer burger (or elk, buffalo, etc.)
50 large yellow onions, chopped
4 cups jalapeño chiles with juice
4 cups canned tomatoes with juice
4 cups chili powder
$^1/_4$ cup Accent
$^1/_4$ cup garlic powder
4 tablespoons cumin
4 tablespoons seasoning salt
4 tablespoons Greek seasoning
Black pepper to taste

In a very large cooking kettle, soak the beans in water for at least 12 hours or overnight. Bring the soaked beans to a boil in the water they soaked in and boil for about 30 minutes. In another large pot, brown the venison or other wild game burger until all is brown and no pink is showing. After the meat is brown, add it along with the remaining ingredients to the bean pot and simmer for about 8 hours, stirring about every 10 minutes. Add a mixture of half tomato juice and half beer to the soup if more liquid is desired. Take turns checking the soup for seasoning and serve! This soup is very good and will feed up to 1,200 ornery old cusses!

HERBS, SPICES, AND GREAT SEASONINGS FOR
WILD GAME SOUPS AND STEWS

Without a doubt, herbs and spices can add flavor and variety to your wild game soups and stews. I recommend that you use a little at first, add more when you are sure you like the flavor. To substitute dry herbs for fresh, use $1/3$ teaspoon powdered or $1/2$ teaspoon crushed for 1 tablespoon fresh chopped herbs. Some herbs and spices are expensive, so you might want to buy only a few of the less expensive herbs and spices you will use.

Keep in mind herbs and spices lose flavor and can spoil or get buggy if kept in the cabin cupboard longer than a year. If you use herbs and spices slowly, buy small containers, or store them in the freezer.

Here's a reference list of herbs, spices, and seasonings to use as a guide:

Allspice: great in soups and stews cooked with venison, game birds, and fish.

Basil: great in soups and stews cooked with tomato base.

Bay leaves: great in soups and stews cooked with tomato base, fish, and strong game meats such as muskrat or porcupine.

Black pepper: highly recommended in all soups and stews.

Celery seed: great in soups and stews using pheasant, duck, and most game birds.

Chili powder: a must have for chili soup.

Chives: very good in soups and stews with a milk base. I also like chives with turtle.

Cilantro (coriander leaves): great taste with soups and stews using game birds, fish, or soups with a tomato base.

Cinnamon: gives a blast of flavor to soups and stews using wild boar or bear meat.

Cloves: another goodie to use with wild boar, bear meat, and soups made with a tomato base.

Coriander seed: very good in most stews and helps with wild boar, bear, and duck.

Cumin: great in soups and stews using wild goat, rabbit, squirrel, venison, bear, and turtle.

Dill weed: a blast of flavor in most seafood soups and stews.

Garlic: you name it—diced, minced, pressed, chopped, and in powder form—garlic rules in my cabin!

Ginger (fresh or ground): try it in venison, game bird, wild boar, and put a dab in most small-game recipes.

Italian seasoning: this seasoning is a mixture of marjoram, oregano, basil, and rosemary. I use Italian seasoning in most of my favorite soups and stews because I love the arrangement of flavors.

Marjoram: very good in seafood, game bird, and cheesy soups and stews.

Mint: I love to use mint with wild boar, rabbit, groundhog, beaver, and wild goat.

Mustard: very good in most wild game red meat and fish soups and stews.

Onion: any soup or stew where onion flavor is desired; can be used fresh or dried (minced or powder).

Oregano: an outstanding flavor booster in most stews, chilies, and tomato-base soups.

Paprika: you name it.

Parsley: good in just about every soup or stew; adds color plus highlights wild game.

Rosemary: a champion with most wild game meats and fish.

Thyme: good with fish, upland and game birds, and a great flavor booster with small game.

If you want to cut back on salt intake, try using herbs and spices to season your soups. You will find that you can cut down on the amount of salt you use.

Air drying: Tie small bunches of herbs with string and hang them upside down by the stems in a warm, dry spot out of direct sunlight. Be sure air circulates freely around the bunches. Let dry until the leaves are brittle. This usually takes a few days to a week, depending on the thickness of the leaves. Pick off the dried leaves and store in tightly covered containers in a cool, dry place about two weeks or until dry and brittle.

Microwave drying: Pick the herbs when the dew has just dried. Put them on paper towels on a plate in the microwave. Cook on high for a minute to start (at the point they appear "wet"). Stir, and cook again for another 60 seconds; toss and cook again for about 30 seconds, or until the herbs are dry and crumbly. Rub the herbs between your hands and break up; pick out any twiggy parts and put in small jars or baggies.

Freezing herbs: Wrap in foil or plastic wrap. You can also chop clean herbs, place them in ice cube trays, and fill with water. When needed, remove herb ice cubes and drop into hot cooking liquid. Or you can wrap bunches of fresh herbs in foil or plastic wrap and freeze them for several weeks. You should expect some discoloration of frozen herbs. Mark the date on the container of your dried herbs. They can be kept for one year. Heat, moisture, and light rob herbs of their flavor. Keep in mind you can also make herb butters and herb vinegars, which are great in wild game soups and stews!

CHAPTER TWO

SOUPS AND STEWS USING SMALL GAME

Cookin' soups with the little critters, yeah, buddy. In this chapter we are going to be cookin' soups and stews made with rabbit, squirrel, muskrat, alligator, beaver, opossum, raccoon, armadillo, porcupine, turtle, and a few other little critters!

But before we get started, I want to give you a few good tips to use when cooking wild game soups and stews.

- Vegetables added to a game soup taste better if you sauté them in a little butter first.
- Wild game–tasting fat can be removed from hot soup by floating a large lettuce leaf on the surface.
- You can eliminate wild game–tasting fat from soup and stew by dropping ice cubes into the pot. As you stir, the fat will cling to the cubes. Discard the cubes before they melt and make your vittles cold.
- Another way to remove wild game–tasting fat from your soups or stews is to transfer the soup into a bowl or similar container. Place in the refrigerator overnight. The fat will settle on the surface and turn solid, which is very easily removed by hand. Of course this is only good if you have the time.

- You can camouflage the burnt taste from your game soups and stews by pouring the liquid gently and carefully into a clean pan and flavoring it with curry powder, mustard, or some chutney.
- If you got carried away with the salt, place a raw potato in the bowl, and it will absorb the extra salt.
- Want thicker soup? Try putting instant mashed potatoes and gravy in it. Stir thoroughly and keep adding as much desired.
- A cold wild game soup should always be thoroughly chilled. Prepare and refrigerate the day before, if you can. When serving a cold game soup, chill the bowls or cups you are going to serve it in. The soup will remain cold longer.

When small-game carcasses arrive in the kitchen, examine them carefully for shot holes. A plug of hair that the shot has passed into the meat often marks shot holes. Use a knife point or forceps to probe each shot hole for embedded pellets. Remove dirt and fragments of broken bone. Trim off bloodshot meat. Disjoint carcasses. Refrigerate, freeze, or prepare for cooking immediately. If you want to soak it in salt or vinegar, always refrigerate it while soaking. I was once asked if animals of different ages require different preparation. Often one hears that old animals are tough and young ones are tender. So how does one tell an old animal from a young one? It is difficult for most hunters to tell the age of wild animals, but size is an important factor for determining the age of certain species such as beaver. Knowledge of teeth, bones, feather patterns, and other parts are required. Most small game is less than a year old as most animals die in their first year. For example, did you know that about 80 percent of all quail usually die before they are a year old? Don't worry too much about whether your game is going to be tender or tough; do a good job with the preparation and it will make darn good eatin' soup and stew vittles!

Rob Russell's Squirrel Stew

Old Cousin Rob, keepin' Cousin Rick's dollars in check!

2 squirrels, cleaned and cut into pieces
$^1/_4$ cup flour
1 teaspoon salt
$^1/_2$ teaspoon black pepper
2 tablespoons olive oil
3 cloves garlic, minced
2 large yellow onions, chopped
4 cups water
5 chicken bouillon cubes
1 large baking potato, cubed
2 carrots, chopped
2 ribs celery, chopped
2 cups frozen lima beans
3 cups canned tomatoes, diced
2 cups frozen sweet corn
1 tablespoon Worcestershire sauce
1 teaspoon sugar
3 tablespoons flour

Dredge the squirrel meat pieces in flour, salt, and pepper. Heat the oil and garlic in a large pot or Dutch oven and brown the squirrel meat on all sides. Add the onions and cook until they are tender. Add the water, bouillon cubes, potato, carrots, and celery. Cover and simmer for another 60 minutes. Add the lima beans, tomatoes, sweet corn, Worcestershire sauce, and sugar. Cover and simmer on low for about 30 more minutes. Mix 3 tablespoons flour with about $^1/_2$ cup cold water, stirring until smooth. Add this flour mixture to the stew and simmer until the stew starts to thicken, stirring often. Check the stew for seasoning and serve hot.

Kim Vicker's Old-Fashioned Squirrel Stew

I squirrel, cut into serving-sized pieces
Flour
Seasoned salt and pepper
3 tablespoons butter
7 cups boiling water
I teaspoon thyme
I cup corn
3 potatoes, cubed
$^1/_4$ teaspoon cayenne pepper
3 yellow onions, sliced
2 cups canned tomatoes with juice

Roll the squirrel meat in flour, seasoned salt, and pepper. Brown the meat in butter in a large saucepot. Add the remaining ingredients except the tomatoes, cover, and simmer for about 2 hours. Add the tomatoes and simmer for another 60 minutes. Check the stew for seasoning and serve hot.

Travis Richard's Bunny Stew

1 rabbit, cut up into serving-sized pieces
$^1/_2$ cup flour
3 tablespoons butter
1 cup chopped celery
2 onions, thinly sliced
1 teaspoon seasoned salt
1 teaspoon salt
$^1/_4$ teaspoon white pepper
1 bay leaf
4 cups water
4 cups dry red wine
2 cups chopped diced carrots
4 potatoes, peeled and diced
4 ounces sliced mushrooms, sautéed
$^1/_4$ cup flour
$^1/_4$ cup water

Dredge the rabbit pieces with $^1/_2$ cup flour. Melt the butter in a Dutch oven over medium heat; brown the rabbit meat on all sides. Add the celery, onion, salt, pepper, bay leaf, 4 cups water, and wine; bring to a boil. Reduce the heat to a simmer, cover, and simmer the stew for about 3 hours. Add the carrots, potatoes, and mushrooms; cook for about 30 minutes longer, or until the vegetables are tender. Combine the $^1/_4$ cup flour and the $^1/_4$ cup water; stir until well blended and smooth. Stir the flour mixture into the broth; cook and stir until the stew begins to thicken. Check for seasonings and serve.

RABBIT AND HARE

The rabbit and hare family is a relatively large one, which is just as well. Perhaps more weight in rabbits is shot as game than in all other species of animals combined. The cottontail (2 to 3 pounds) is found all over the country. The swamp or marsh rabbit of the Southeast has webbed hind feet and is an excellent swimmer; it can weigh around 3 pounds. The snowshoe rabbit called the varying hare because of its seasonal color changes and the jackrabbit are also popularly hunted species ranging from 4 to 10 pounds. The arctic, at around 12 pounds, is the largest. Rabbits are generally good eating and make some great-tasting soups and stews, but they are notoriously susceptible to becoming hosts for tularemia. Young specimens are always the best eating, although the snowshoe and the jackrabbit are a bit sinewy to start with, even at an early age. Moist cooking is the best treatment for these. Cottontails, particularly young ones, have moist white meat and also make excellent soup and stew meat. I have found that rabbit meat can be prepared the same as chicken. It is mild-flavored, fine-grained, and practically all white meat. Rabbit meat should always be cooked until well done. Remember most rabbits weigh from 2 to 6 pounds, and young and tender ones can be cooked the same as young and tender chickens. Most young rabbits do not require soaking in strong salt water to tenderize them.

Hare In My Stew

> 1 frozen, dressed rabbit
> 1 large yellow onion, chopped
> 1 green bell pepper, diced
> 2 stalks celery, sliced
> 2 cloves garlic, chopped
> Salt and pepper
> $^1/_2$ teaspoon oregano
> 1 tablespoon dried parsley
> 2 carrots, chopped
> 3 tablespoons tomato paste
> $^1/_4$ teaspoon cayenne pepper
> 1 cup white wine, or cider
> Marinade ($^1/_2$ cup vinegar, 2 tablespoons salt, 1 tablespoon minced garlic)

Defrost the rabbit meat for 10 hours in the marinade. Brown the rabbit meat with the vegetables in a hot skillet. Place the cooked rabbit and the remaining ingredients in a large slow cooker, cover and cook on low heat for about 12 hours.

Montrose Muskrat Stew

I muskrat, cleaned and cut into pieces
Flour seasoned with seasoned salt and pepper to taste
3 tablespoons butter
6 cups boiling water
I cup dark beer
I teaspoon thyme
I cup kernel corn
3 cubed potatoes
$^1/_2$ teaspoon cayenne pepper
3 medium red onions, sliced
I tablespoon Accent
2 cups canned tomatoes with juice

Roll the muskrat pieces in the seasoned flour and brown in butter in a large pot. Add the remaining ingredients except the tomatoes and cook, covered, for about 2 hours. Add the tomatoes and simmer, uncovered, for about 30 minutes more. Check the stew for seasoning and serve.

Wally's Gator Jambalaya

I cup green bell pepper, chopped
2 cloves garlic, crushed
$^3/_4$ cup parsley
I cup celery, chopped
3 cups canned tomatoes, with juice
2 cups chicken broth
I cup green onion, chopped
I pound marinated alligator fillet cut into small bite-sized chunks
I pound Italian sausage
3 tablespoons olive oil
2 teaspoons oregano
I teaspoon Frank's Red Hot Sauce
I teaspoon Cajun spice
Salt and pepper to taste
2 cups raw white rice

In a deep frying pan, sauté the bell peppers, garlic, parsley, and celery. While this is cooking, add the tomatoes and juices, the chicken broth, and green onions to a large pot. Stir in the remaining ingredients and simmer on low heat for about 2 hours. Check for seasonings and serve hot. Make sure to stir often so ingredients do not stick to the bottom of the pan.

Argyle Hills Raccoon Stew

5 pounds raccoon meat, cut into cubes
3 white onions, sliced
3 cups canned tomatoes, chopped
Salt and pepper to taste
1 bay leaf
1 teaspoon Worcestershire sauce
$^1/_2$ cup carrots, chopped
4 large baking potatoes, cubed
1 turnip, cubed

Brown the meat cubes slowly in a Dutch oven. There should be enough fat within the tissues that no additional oil will be needed. Add the onions during the last browning process so they won't become scorched. Reduce the heat, add enough tomatoes and tomato juice to cover the meat, season and cover. Simmer on low heat until the meat is tender. Add the remaining ingredients and simmer on low, stirring often for about 2 hours, or until all is tender. Check for seasoning before serving.

RACCOON

Raccoons should have all the fat, inside and out, removed, as well as the glands that are under the legs, along the spine, and in the small of the back. The meat is very dark, long fibered, and somewhat coarse; it is improved by an hour's parboiling before continuing with a recipe. Young ones, 7 to 8 pounds, can be marinated overnight in 1 tablespoon of salt per 1 quart of water. Older ones, up to 15 pounds, should be marinated for at least 24 hours.

Whiskey Breath Betty's Hot Snapping Turtle Stew

2 tablespoons butter
2 pounds snapping turtle meat, chopped into 1-inch cubes
1 white onion, sliced
2 cups celery, chopped, including the greens
1 cup lima beans, soaked in salt water for at least 8 hours
3 potatoes, diced
1 cup canned potatoes
$1/2$ cup chopped parsley
$1/2$ cup chopped red bell pepper
3 tablespoons cooking sherry

Melt the butter in a large skillet and brown the turtle meat on all sides. Remove the cooked meat from skillet. Add 2 quarts of water and bring to a boil. Reduce the heat and add the cooked turtle meat and the remaining ingredients. Simmer on low heat, covered, for about 45 minutes, or until all vegetables are tender. Check the stew for seasoning and serve hot.

Camp Kill-a-Kritter Beaver Stew

1 pound beaver roast, cut into thin strips
Butter
2 cups canned whole tomatoes, diced
1 cup beer
1 large baking potato, diced
1 large white onion, diced
1 cup canned garbanzo beans
Seasoning salt and pepper to taste

In a large skillet brown the beaver meat in butter. Add the remaining ingredients and bring to a boil. Reduce the heat, cover, and simmer for about 70 minutes. Check the stew for seasoning and serve.

Stony Hollow Tree Rat Gumbo

4 squirrels, cleaned
1 chicken
2 cups green bell pepper, chopped
2 cups celery, chopped
1 large white onion, chopped
1 quart stewed tomatoes
$^1/_2$ cup tomato sauce
2 cups canned okra
3 tablespoons creole gumbo seasoning
$^3/_4$ cup dark roux

Pressure-cook and debone the squirrels and chicken. Save the juices. In a large pot or kettle, bring the meat juices to a boil and add the bell peppers, celery, onions, tomatoes, and tomato sauce. Make the roux using oil and flour in equal parts; in a heavy skillet brown the roux and add to the gumbo mixture, stirring until well blended. Cook until the vegetables are tender. Add the cooked meat and okra. Simmer for another 30 minutes on low heat and serve.

LEAVE IT TO BEAVER

Beaver meat is much like that of the muskrat. The flesh is dark, fine-grained, tender, and soft. This animal also has kernels or scent glands that are found between the forelegs, under the thighs, and along the spine in the small of the back. They should be removed immediately after the skin has been removed. Take care not to cut into them. Beaver fat has a very strong flavor and odor and should also be completely stripped off before cooking. I have found that you can make beaver meat milder in flavor by covering the meat in water; bring to a boil and then add 1 tablespoon each of baking soda and black pepper. I simmer the meat for about 20 minutes, drain, and then use in my soups and stews.

Muscatine Swamp Muskrat Soup

1 muskrat
Rich milk
3 hard-boiled eggs
1 tablespoon dry mustard
1 tablespoon flour
3 tablespoons cooking sherry
Cayenne pepper, black pepper, and seasoning salt to taste

In a large soup pot, cover the meat in water and cook slowly until tender, adding water if needed. Cool and take the meat from the bones and cut into small pieces using meat scissors. Save the liquid from the pot and add an equal amount of rich milk. Mash the egg yolks, add mustard and flour, and stir the broth into it. Season to taste with the seasonings. Chop the egg whites and add the egg whites and meat to the soup after it has boiled. Add the cooking sherry, stir, and serve hot.

Swatch Creek Beaver Stew

$^1/_2$ cup flour
1 teaspoon seasoned salt
1 teaspoon white pepper
2 yellow onions, sliced
3 pounds beaver meat, cut in 1-inch cubes
Bacon fat
2 tablespoons sugar
$^1/_2$ teaspoon thyme
$^1/_2$ teaspoon tarragon
$^1/_2$ pound carrots, chopped
6 potatoes, diced
Beer
2 garlic cloves, minced

Combine the flour, seasoned salt, and pepper in a plastic closable container and shake until all is mixed well. Add the beaver meat and shake until all the meat is well coated. Dice the onions. Melt enough bacon fat in the bottom of a skillet to sauté the onions and beaver meat. Sauté the onions and coated meat in the bacon fat, adding more fat as needed. Place the sautéed meat and onions in a cooking pot with enough water to cover. Add the remaining ingredients and simmer. Add about 1 cup of beer to the skillet where the beaver meat and onions cooked and deglaze the pan; pour this pan gravy into the stew. This stew is ready for serving when the vegetables and meat are all tender. Check the stew for seasoning and serve hot.

Iowa Beaver Stew

I large beaver
Buttermilk
I bay leaf
2 yellow onions
2 garlic cloves
$^1/_2$ celery leaves
5 diced carrots
I tablespoon sugar
2 teaspoons thyme
Flour
Garlic salt and pepper
Bacon fat

Remove all the fat from the beaver. Cut up into small stew-sized pieces. Soak the meat overnight in salt water. Marinate the meat for 8 hours in buttermilk. Parboil until the meat is about half-cooked in water with the bay leaf, onions, garlic, celery, carrot, and seasonings. Drain, roll the meat in flour and brown on all sides in bacon fat; season with salt and pepper. Bake in a covered pan in a 350-degree oven for about 45 minutes, or until the meat is tender. Make gravy from the drippings. Add this gravy to the beaver stew meat and serve.

Slappy Gibbon's Carolina Beaver Stew Vittles

4 pounds beaver leg and back meat, cut into 1-inch cubes

Brine (4 cups water, 2 teaspoons salt, and 2 teaspoons cider vinegar)

$^1/_2$ cup mushrooms, chopped

Flour

8 ounces thick-cut smoked bacon, chopped

1 white onion, diced

1 cup celery, diced

1 cup carrots, diced

1 cup vegetable juice

2 cups beef broth

1 cup beer

6 ounces salad oil

1 tablespoon Holland Grill seasoning salt

1 teaspoon black pepper

Soak the beaver meat in the brine solution for at least 2 hours. Drain the brine. Soak the mushrooms in a cup of hot water for about 15 minutes. Toss the beaver meat in flour. Heat oil in a large pan and brown the beaver meat on all sides. Place the meat in a large glass baking bowl. Pour off the fat from the pan and add the bacon, cooking until crispy. Add the vegetables and mushrooms, and cook all until tender. Add the vegetables and all remaining ingredients to the baking bowl with the meat and stir. Bake the stew in the oven at 350 degrees for about 60 minutes, or until all is tender. Check the stew for seasoning and serve hot.

Uncle Mike Black's Florida Alligator Trooper's Stew

To serve and protect! Unless you're a tasty gator!

1 leek, sliced
3 garlic cloves, minced
1 tablespoon dried tarragon
$^1/_2$ teaspoon grated lemon peel
$^1/_2$ teaspoon thyme
$^1/_2$ teaspoon black pepper
$^1/_2$ teaspoon dried sage
3 pounds alligator, cut into 1-inch cubes
1 cup seasoned flour
1 cup white wine
$^1/_2$ cup lemon juice
1 tablespoon cornstarch
Cream

In a large slow cooker, combine the leek, garlic, tarragon, lemon peel, thyme, black pepper, and sage. Coat the meat cubes with seasoned flour and then add to the crock. Pour in the wine and lemon juice. Cover and cook on low setting for about 8 hours, or until the meat is tender. In a small mixing bowl, mix cornstarch with cream and blend into the stew. Increase the heat and cook for another 20 minutes, stirring often. Check the stew for seasoning and serve.

POSSUM

The opossum is a very fat animal with peculiarly flavored meat. It is dressed much as one would dress a suckling pig, removing the entrails and, if desired, the head and tail. After it has been dressed, wash it thoroughly inside and out with hot water. Cover with a solution of cold water and 1 cup of salt. Allow it to stand overnight in the refrigerator; in the morning, drain off the salt water and rinse the meat well with clear, boiling water.

Major Schmidt's Alligator Stew

$1/2$ cup vegetable oil
I quart alligator meat, diced
$1/2$ cup chopped red onion
$1/2$ cup chopped red bell pepper
$1/2$ cup chopped celery
2 tablespoons minced parsley
2 cups canned tomatoes with green chiles
I cup beef stock
I cup beer
3 cups cooked white rice

In a heavy cooking pot, add all the ingredients except the rice and cook, covered, for about 60 minutes on medium heat, or until the meat is tender. Season with salt and pepper to taste and serve stew over hot cooked rice.

Konawa River Valley Turtle Soup

I large smoked ham steak
2 garlic cloves, minced
I teaspoon thyme
I teaspoon parsley
2 pounds turtle meat
I chopped onion
Bacon fat
2 tablespoons flour
I bay leaf
I tablespoon lemon zest
3 quarts beef stock
Garlic salt and pepper to taste

Cut the ham steak into small bite-sized chunks; mash the herbs and seasonings with it, and set aside. Boil the turtle meat for about 20 minutes. Remove from the heat and save the stock. Chop up the meat. In a large pot, brown the onions in bacon fat; add the turtle meat and brown well. Add the ham and seasonings, stirring constantly. Add the remaining ingredients and simmer for about 60 minutes or until all is tender and seasoned well.

Sweet Armadillo Soup

I pound ground armadillo meat, cooked and drained
I cup chopped onions
2 garlic cloves, minced
I green chile, minced
3 cups vegetable stock
2 teaspoons ground cumin
2 cups sweet potatoes, cubed
3 cups fresh or frozen corn kernels
1/2 cup diced red bell pepper
Salt and pepper to taste

Toss the cooked armadillo meat, onions, garlic, and chile in a soup pot with the vegetable stock and simmer for about 10 minutes. Add the cumin and sweet potatoes and simmer for another 10 minutes, or until the sweet potatoes are tender. Add the corn and red bell peppers. Simmer for another 10 minutes. Check the soup for seasoning and serve.

HARD OF HEARING

An old squirrel hunter goes to the doctor for his yearly physical with his wife tagging along. When the doctor enters the examination room, he tells the old hunter, "I need a urine and a stool sample." The old hunter, being hard of hearing, looks at his wife and yells, "What's he want?" His wife yells back, "He wants your underwear."

Tree Top Timber Stew

2 pounds porcupine meat, cubed

$^1/_2$ cup ketchup

$^1/_4$ cup brown sugar

I teaspoon salt

$^1/_2$ cup chopped celery

$^1/_4$ cup cooking oil

I cup beef stock

$^1/_4$ cup vinegar

I tablespoon Worcestershire sauce

I sliced onion

I cup canned carrots, drained

Combine all the ingredients except the meat and carrots in a saucepot and simmer on low heat for about 30 minutes. This will make the stew sauce. Brown the meat and remove from skillet. Place the meat in a baking dish. Pour the sauce over the meat and bake at 325 degrees for about 30 minutes. Add the carrots and bake for another 20 minutes. Check the stew for seasoning and serve.

Ozark Possum Hillbilly Stew

4 pounds possum meat, cubed

4 tablespoons oil

2 garlic cloves, chopped

4 cups hot water

4 cups canned tomatoes

2 thin slices of lemon

4 sliced white onions

2 tablespoons seasoned salt

$^1/_2$ teaspoon white pepper

6 tablespoons sugar

12 carrots, peeled and cut into I inch pieces

10 medium potatoes, quartered

$^1/_2$ teaspoon dried basil leaves

2 cups English peas

In a skillet, brown the possum meat well in oil. When cooked, transfer to a large Dutch oven and mix in the garlic. Add the hot water, tomatoes, lemon, onions, seasoned salt, pepper, and sugar. Mix well and simmer for about 2 hours, stirring occasionally. Add the carrots, potatoes, and crushed basil leaves. Cover and cook until the vegetables are tender. Add the peas and simmer for another 30 minutes. If necessary, thicken with flour dissolved in water. Serve hot.

Take Me Back To Old Virginia Squirrel Soup

1 stick butter

1 cup flour

2 quarts vegetable stock

2 pounds squirrel meat, diced

1 cup coarsely chopped onions

1 cup sliced carrots

1 cup sliced celery

2 cups frozen mixed vegetables

2 cups canned tomatoes

1 tablespoon monosodium glutamate

2 tablespoons granulated instant beef bouillon

1 teaspoon ground black pepper

In a very large soup pot (at least 1 gallon), melt the butter and whip in flour to make a smooth paste. Heat until bubbly; then stir in vegetable stock until all lumps are gone. Continue cooking until the mixture comes to a boil, and then reduce heat to a simmer. Meanwhile, brown the squirrel meat in a skillet, drain off any fat, and add the meat to the soup liquid. Add the onions, carrots, and celery to the soup and simmer for another 30 minutes. Add the remaining ingredients and simmer for about 20 minutes more, making sure all the vegetables are cooked and tender.

Old Nauvoo Quick Muskrat Stew

Old Joe would be proud!

2 pounds muskrat meat, diced
Oil
1 teaspoon salt
1 teaspoon pepper
1 cup carrots, sliced
$^1/_2$ cup celery
1 cup tomato soup
1 cup water
1 large potato, peeled and sliced
1 bay leaf (remove after cooking)

In a skillet, brown the muskrat in oil until all sides of meat are dark brown. Season the meat with salt and pepper and set aside. Place all the remaining ingredients including the cooked meat in a large casserole dish with a tight-fitting lid. Bake at 275 degrees for about 5 hours.

MUSKRATS

Another true furbearer, the muskrat (also known in restaurants and in some areas as "marsh rabbit," although there is a true swamp or marsh rabbit) is noted for its clean food habits. It's a vegetarian and, as such, seldom eats anything to give an offensive flavor to its dark meat. But it can carry tularemia. The fat is unpleasant and should be removed. This is most easily done if the skinned and cleaned carcass (it has musk glands, too, which should be removed) is refrigerated overnight. This hardens the fat and makes it easier to peel off.

Bubba Clark's Coon Stew

3 pounds raccoon stew meat, cut into bite-sized pieces

2 large onions, chopped

2 cloves garlic, minced

1 tablespoon Worcestershire sauce

$^1/_3$ cup dry red wine

$^1/_3$ cup all-purpose flour

2 tablespoons sugar

1 teaspoon dried thyme

$^1/_2$ teaspoon black pepper

4 cups beef broth

1 12-ounce can beer

4 large potatoes, cut into 1-inch cubes

5 large carrots, sliced $^1/_2$ inch thick

2 cups coarsely chopped cabbage

$^3/_4$ cup coarsely chopped celery

2 bay leaves

Salt to taste

Combine the meat, onions, garlic, and Worcestershire sauce in a large pot. Cover and cook over medium heat for about 30 minutes. Uncover and stir often until the liquid evaporates. Add the wine and stir to release browned bits. Mix the flour, sugar, thyme, and pepper with one cup broth. Add the beer, potatoes, carrots, cabbage, celery, and bay leaves. Cover and simmer until the meat is very tender and the vegetables are cooked. Season to taste with salt.

Autumn Winds Rabbit Stew

2 pounds rabbit meat, sliced thin
8 large carrots
5 large onions
5 large potatoes
2 sticks butter
Garlic powder
Salt
Pepper

Place the rabbit meat in a Dutch oven as the first layer. Cut up the carrots, onions, and potatoes, and layer them in the Dutch oven. After you finish, slice up 1 stick of butter and cover the vegetables. Then, season with garlic powder, salt, and pepper. Repeat the layers, starting with the rabbit meat again. Cook in Dutch oven until the rabbit is tender and the vegetables are cooked.

Stoker Farms Beaver Soup

3 tablespoons cooking oil
1 pound beaver roast, cut into 1/8-inch pieces
1 teaspoon salt
1 large onion, chopped
1 pound baking potatoes, peeled and diced
1/2 pound green beans, ends trimmed
2 cups water
1 quart chicken broth
1/4 teaspoon black pepper
2 teaspoons Worcestershire sauce

In a large pot, heat 1 tablespoon of the oil over moderately high heat. Add the half of the beaver meat and cook, stirring frequently, until well browned. Remove the meat with a slotted spoon. Repeat with another tablespoon of oil and the remaining meat. Remove the meat from the pot and toss all of the cooked meat with 1/4 teaspoon of the salt. Reduce the heat to moderately low and add the remaining tablespoon of oil to the pot. Add the onion and cook, stirring occasionally, until translucent. Add the potatoes, green beans, water, broth, the remaining salt, and the black pepper to the pot. Bring to a boil, scraping the bottom of the pot with a spoon to dislodge browned bits. Reduce the heat and simmer until the potatoes are tender. Return the beaver meat and any juices to the soup and stir in the Worcestershire sauce. With this soup it is very important to make sure the meat is well browned before removing it from the pot; those brown bits left in the bottom are essential for flavoring the broth.

Willard Ohio Squirrel Stew

1 squirrel, cut in 7 pieces
Flour
Salt to taste
Freshly ground black pepper to taste
3 tablespoons butter
7 cups boiling chicken stock
1 teaspoon thyme
1 cup corn
1 cup sweet peas
3 potatoes, cubed
$^{1}/_{2}$ teaspoon cayenne pepper
3 medium white onions, chopped
3 cups vegetable juice

Roll the squirrel pieces in flour, salt, and pepper. Brown in butter and add the squirrel and all the remaining ingredients to a large pot. Cover the pot and simmer for about 3 hours. Check the stew for seasoning and serve hot.

Swamp Breath Byron's Alligator Stew

3 tablespoons flour

$^1/_2$ teaspoon cumin

$^1/_2$ teaspoon chili powder

$^1/_2$ teaspoon cinnamon

2 pounds alligator meat, cut into 1-inch cubes

2 tablespoons olive oil

1 tablespoon butter

4 cloves garlic, minced

1 cup chicken stock

$^1/_2$ cup orange juice

6 red potatoes, peeled and cubed

2 sweet potatoes, peeled and cubed

1 green bell pepper, diced

1 red bell pepper, diced

1 cup canned tomatoes with green chiles

1 cup tomato sauce

1 cup canned kidney beans, drained

2 tablespoons capers, drained

2 tablespoons fresh cilantro, chopped

Seasoned salt to taste

Black pepper to taste

1 cup shredded cheddar cheese

In a large mixing bowl, combine the flour, cumin, chili powder, and cinnamon. Add the alligator meat and toss well to coat. In a large heavy pot, heat the olive oil and butter. Add the garlic and sauté for about 2 minutes. Add the meat and sauté for about 3 minutes. Add the chicken stock and orange juice, bring to a boil briefly, and then reduce the heat. Cover and simmer for about 20 minutes. Add the potatoes, sweet potatoes, bell peppers, tomatoes, tomato sauce, and kidney beans. Cover and simmer for about 40 minutes, or until the potatoes are tender. Stir in the capers and chopped cilantro, and season with seasoning salt and pepper. Serve with shredded cheddar on top.

ALLIGATOR

Alligator meat has a very mild taste and readily adapts to recipes for pork, veal, chicken and most seafood. Choice cuts of meat, primarily the tail and jaw, can be used in just about any soup and stew recipe. The seasoned cooks will use mostly the neck and leg meats for alligator soups, stews, and gumbos, which with just a little preparation and special soup recipes can be just as tasty. The meat has a fine, light-grained texture that appeals to most hunters and has its own unique flavor that is easily enhanced with seasonings. If you're like me and don't live where there is fresh alligator meat, make it a point to research and find a wholesale distributor that has a good reputation for handling quality meat.

Lowland Quick Gator Stew

6 cups cream of mushroom soup
2 cups canned mixed vegetables
2 cups canned potatoes
2 pounds, boneless, cooked, alligator meat
Salt and pepper to taste
1 teaspoon dried parsley

Add all the ingredients to a heavy pot. Cover and simmer for about 40 minutes, stirring often. Check the stew for seasoning and serve.

Chef Zigmond Jones's (Pappy) Cajun Alligator Stew

2 tablespoons olive oil

1 cup onions, chopped

$^1/_2$ cup celery, chopped

$^1/_2$ cup green bell peppers, chopped

2 tablespoons garlic, minced

3 cups tomatoes, peeled, seeded, and chopped

$^1/_4$ cup fresh basil, chopped

2 tablespoons fresh oregano

2 teaspoons fresh thyme, chopped

1 teaspoon salt

$^1/_2$ teaspoon cayenne pepper

$^1/_2$ teaspoon white pepper

2 teaspoons Worcestershire sauce

3 cups chicken broth

2 cups chopped green onions

1 pound alligator meat, cut into stew-sized pieces

1 tablespoon Louisiana hot sauce

In a large saucepan, heat the oil. When the oil is hot, sauté the onions, celery, and peppers. When the vegetables are tender, add the garlic, tomatoes, basil, oregano, and thyme. Simmer all for about 3 minutes and add the remaining ingredients. Bring the stew to a boil, cover, and reduce the heat to a simmer. Cook on low for about 20 minutes, stirring every 5 minutes. Check the meat and the vegetables for tenderness. Serve hot in small bowls or over your favorite toasted French bread.

Montrose Turtle Soup

Montrose, Iowa, home of the watermelon feast and the widest part of the Mississippi River!

10 pounds turtle meat, boneless
8 pounds chicken meat, with bones
8 pounds pork roast, boneless
8 large onions, chopped
6 pounds red potatoes, peeled, cubed
2 cups butter
2 quarts half-and-half
2 gallons milk
Salt and pepper to taste

Place the turtle, chicken, and pork meat into separate pots with enough water to cover each of the meats. Bring each pot to a boil, and cook until tender. Discard the water from the turtle and pork, but save the chicken stock. Debone the chicken, cut all of the meat into stew-sized pieces, and set aside. In a very large stockpot, combine the turtle, chicken, and pork meat, onions, and reserved chicken stock. Bring to a boil and cook until the onions are tender. Season to taste with the salt and pepper. Add the potatoes and butter to the stockpot, and cook for about 40 minutes, or until the potatoes are tender but not soft. Reduce the heat to a low simmer. Stir in the half-and-half and milk. Bring the soup to a simmer, stirring often, for about 20 minutes. Serve the soup hot with Vista Bakery saltines.

Armadillo Soup Grub

$^1/_2$ pound armadillo stew meat, chopped

I teaspoon vegetable oil

I cup thinly sliced carrots

I cup thinly sliced potatoes

2 I-ounce packages dry onion soup mix

2 tablespoons sugar

4 cups water

I 28-ounce can crushed tomatoes

$^1/_4$ teaspoon Italian seasoning

$^1/_4$ teaspoon hot pepper sauce

$^1/_2$ cup seashell pasta

Ground black pepper to taste

In a large stockpot, heat the oil over medium heat; add the meat and brown. Stir in the carrots, potatoes, onion soup mix, sugar, water, tomatoes, Italian seasoning, hot pepper sauce, and pepper. Stir frequently. Bring to a boil, add the pasta, and reduce heat. Simmer gently for about 40 minutes, or until the vegetables are tender. Check for seasoning and serve hot.

Adam Baum's Turtle Stew

2 pounds turtle meat

2 quarts water

Flour

4 tablespoons butter

I garlic clove, pressed

I large yellow onion, chopped

I cup potatoes, diced

2 cups tomato soup

Cut the turtle meat into bite-sized pieces and boil in 2 quarts water for about 25 minutes. Remove the meat, let it cool, and lightly roll it in flour. Save stock. In a Dutch oven, melt the butter, add the garlic, and cook slowly until lightly browned. Add the onion and lightly floured turtle meat, carefully turning until golden brown. Pour about 4 cups of the stock over the meat and simmer for about 3 hours, or until the meat is tender. Add the diced potatoes, tomato soup, and the remaining stock. Simmer the soup for another 45 minutes, check for seasoning, and serve hot.

Doc McCabe's Otter Island Turtle Soup

3 pints water, seasoned with 1 tablespoon sea salt

1 pound turtle meat

2 cups tomato soup

1 chopped white onion

1 chopped celery stalk

1 chopped green bell pepper

1 cup barley

1 teaspoon salt

2 tablespoons Worcestershire sauce

2 teaspoons lemon juice

$1/2$ cup dry red wine

Bring the 3 salted pints of water to a boil in a large stockpot. Add the turtle meat, tomato soup, and vegetables, and cook for about 60 minutes. Add the barley; cook 30 minutes more. Add the remaining ingredients and simmer for about 30 minutes. Check for seasoning and serve hot.

KT's Turtle Soup

2 pounds turtle meat
2 tablespoons shortening
I cup chopped white onion
2 stalks celery, chopped
I green bell pepper, diced
I bay leaf
I sprig thyme
4 tablespoons tomato paste
Salt and pepper to taste
3 tablespoons flour
I quart hot water
I cup red wine
2 hard-boiled eggs, sliced
I sliced lemon

Cut the turtle meat into soup-sized pieces and fry them in the shortening until brown. Add the onions, celery, green pepper, bay leaf, thyme, tomato paste, salt, pepper, and flour. Stir well. Add water and simmer for about 2 hours. Remove from heat and add the wine. Check the soup for seasoning. Serve the soup with sliced egg and lemon in each bowl.

Dewey Needham's Emu Goulash

I stick of butter
3 sliced onions
I tablespoon paprika
6 ounces tomato paste
I ounce vinegar
2 cups beef broth
2 pounds emu meat cut into cubes
$1/4$ teaspoon sugar
$1/4$ teaspoon minced garlic
Cooked noodles or rice
Cottage cheese

Melt the butter in a large pot with cover, add all of the ingredients except noodles, rice, and cottage cheese. Stir, cover, and cook for about 4 hours, or until the soup becomes thick. Check for seasoning and serve hot over cooked noodles or rice with a dab of cottage cheese on top.

"Hey Mate" Kangaroo Tail Soup

1 kangaroo tail
Butter
3 carrots
3 onions
2 pounds venison
1 bunch herbs (cook's choice)
Salt and pepper to taste

Cut the kangaroo tail into joints and fry in butter until golden brown. Slice the vegetables and fry them in the butter until crisp. Cut the venison meat into thin slices and boil for about 4 hours in 3 quarts of water. Remove all pieces of the tailbone. Strain the stock and thicken with flour. Add all the ingredients back to the stock and simmer for 30 minutes. Check the soup for seasoning and serve.

Rascally Rabbit Stew

1 pound ground rabbit meat (bunny burger)
16 ounces canned pinto beans
4 ounces canned sliced jalapeño peppers
15 ounces canned kidney beans
15 ounces canned yellow wax beans
16 ounces canned baked beans with pork
18 ounces BBQ sauce
28 ounces canned peeled tomatoes
6 ounces tomato paste
$1/2$ cup brown sugar

Place the bunny burger in a large, deep skillet. Cook over medium heat until evenly brown. Drain, crumble, and set aside. Preheat the oven to 350 degrees. In a large ovenproof pot or Dutch oven, combine cooked bunny burger, pinto beans, peppers, kidney beans, wax beans, baked beans, BBQ sauce, tomatoes, tomato paste, and brown sugar. Be sure to add all liquids from canned vegetables. Bake in a preheated oven for about 60 minutes. Check the stew for seasoning before serving hot from the oven.

Toothless Eddie's Green Chile Stew with Squirrel

3 pounds squirrel meat, boneless, diced
3 tablespoons peanut oil
3 stalks celery, chopped
2 tomatoes, chopped
7 green chile peppers, chopped
4 cloves garlic, crushed
4 cups chicken stock
Salt and pepper to taste
1 cup green chile salsa

In a large skillet over medium heat, brown the squirrel meat in oil in 2 to 3 batches. Place the meat in a covered casserole and add the celery, tomatoes, chiles, and garlic. Add about 1 cup chicken stock to the skillet, stirring over high heat to scrape up browned bits on the bottom; bring to a boil. Add to the pot with enough additional stock to barely cover the ingredients. Cover and simmer until the stew is thick and the meat is very tender, about 2 hours. Add salt and pepper to taste just before serving. If you're like me and like your stew hotter, add a tablespoon of jalapeño salsa.

Cousin Rick's Favorite Muskrat Soup

2 tablespoons vegetable oil
$^1/_4$ small head cabbage, shredded
4 ounces muskrat meat, cut into thin strips
6 cups chicken stock
2 tablespoons soy sauce
$^1/_2$ teaspoon minced fresh ginger root
8 fresh green onions, chopped
4 ounces dry Chinese noodles

In a large skillet, heat the oil over medium heat. Add the cabbage and muskrat meat strips; fry until the meat is tender and done, about 6 minutes. Make sure to stir the cabbage and meat while it is cooking. Add the chicken stock, soy sauce, and ginger, and bring to a boil. Reduce the heat to low and simmer for about 15 minutes, stirring occasionally. Stir in the onions and add the noodles. Cook until the noodles are tender. Check the soup for seasoning and serve hot.

Old Melcher Inn's Saturday Evening Rabbit Stew

1 rabbit, cut up fryer

2 onions, cut up

2 bay leaves

1 teaspoon coarse black pepper

1 teaspoon salt

1 teaspoon crushed dried tarragon

1 teaspoon crushed dried thyme

Cold water

4 large carrots, peeled, halved

4 potatoes, peeled, diced

1 cup flour

$^1/_2$ cup ground suet

Salt and pepper to taste

$^1/_4$ cup fresh chopped parsley

2 teaspoons baking powder

Place the meat pieces in a large Dutch oven. Add the onions, bay leaves, pepper, salt, tarragon, and thyme, and cover with water. Cover and cook over medium heat for about 2 hours. Add the carrots and potatoes. In a small bowl, combine flour, suet, salt, pepper, parsley, and baking powder. Add just enough cold water to pull together into soft dough with your hands. Do not kneed or squeeze the dough. Divide into 8 small portions and drop onto the top of the gently boiling cooking liquid. Cook for about 20 minutes. Use a slotted spoon to remove the dumplings and meat pieces; keep warm while you slightly thicken the remaining liquid by adding a little flour. Check the stew and dumplings for seasoning and serve hot.

Bunny Got Creamed

1 large rabbit, cut up
1 cup diced ham
1 finely chopped onion
$^1/_2$ teaspoon leaf thyme
1 cup canned mushrooms, sliced, drained
1 cup beef bouillon
1 cup sour cream
2 tablespoons lemon juice
3 tablespoons flour
Minced parsley

Marinate the rabbit overnight in the refrigerator in salted water. Before cooking, remove the rabbit pieces and pat dry. Place the rabbit, ham, onion, thyme, and mushrooms in a large crock. Pour in the bouillon, cover, and cook on low for about 10 hours. Before serving, turn heat to high. Combine the sour cream, lemon juice, and flour. Remove the rabbit and debone it. Stir the sour cream mixture into the crock and cook until all is thick. Sprinkle in the parsley and rabbit meat. Check stew for seasoning and serve.

Crandall's Wild Rabbit Gumbo

Old Darren gets the "whiskey eyes" and fixes this here great gumbo!

¹/₂ cup flour
¹/₂ cup cooking oil
3 chopped white onions
I chopped green bell pepper
¹/₂ cup chopped celery
Salt and pepper to taste
Frank's Red Hot Sauce to taste
3 quarts chicken stock
I rabbit, cut into pieces
I pint oysters
²/₃ cup chopped shallots
¹/₃ cup chopped parsley

Make a roux using flour and oil. Cook slowly until dark brown, stirring often. Add the onions, bell pepper, and celery, cooking until tender. Add the seasonings and 3 quarts hot chicken stock. Add the rabbit meat and cook in a large covered pot for about 2 hours, or until the rabbit meat is tender. Add the oysters, shallots, and parsley. Simmer slowly until the edges of the oysters begin to curl. Serve gumbo over cooked rice and French bread.

Port Royal Gator Stew

I tablespoon olive oil
2 pounds gator meat, diced
I tablespoon ground cumin
Salt and pepper to taste
3 cups canned white hominy
3 cups chicken stock
20 dried chile de arbol peppers
¹/₄ cup beer
I cup minced white onion
I teaspoon minced garlic

Heat the oil in a large skillet over medium heat; add the diced gator meat, cumin, and salt and pepper to taste. Cook, stirring frequently, until the gator meat is evenly browned. Transfer the meat to a large pot. Stir in the hominy and chicken stock. Cook over medium heat for about an hour. While the soup is cooking, place the chiles in a small saucepan with 2 cups water. Boil for about 45 minutes, covered. Drain and remove the stems. Place the chiles in a blender with $1/4$ cup beer, onion, and garlic. Blend until smooth. Set aside. Serve the soup in bowls with 1 teaspoon of chile sauce in each.

Squirrelly Pepper Stew

$1/2$ **cup bacon drippings**
2 pounds squirrel meat, boneless, cut into $1/2$-inch strips
$1/4$ **cup butter**
3 onions, thinly sliced
2 tablespoons flour
3 tablespoons paprika
I green bell pepper, cut into strips
I red bell pepper, cut into strips
I yellow bell pepper, cut into strips
2 jalapeño peppers, sliced into rings
I cup beef broth
3 tablespoons tomato paste
2 garlic cloves, minced
I teaspoon salt
I bay leaf

Heat the bacon grease in a large pot over medium heat. Stir in the squirrel meat and cook until evenly browned. Remove the meat and liquid from the pot and set aside. Add the butter to the pot and melt. Sauté the onions until they are tender, mix in the flour and paprika, and cook, stirring constantly, until thickened. Mix the meat, green, red, and yellow bell peppers, and jalapeños in the pot. Stir in the beef broth, tomato paste, garlic, salt, and bay leaf. Bring the stew to a boil. Reduce the heat, cover, and simmer for about 2 hours, stirring every 10 minutes or so. Check the stew for seasoning and serve hot.

Cochenour's Squirrel Stew

Samuel Daniel can shoot a tree rat on the run!

I squirrel
3 carrots, diced
3 potatoes, diced
I tablespoon celery salt
I onion, chopped
2 garlic cloves, crushed
I teaspoon sweet basil
$^1/_2$ cup sour cream
$^1/_4$ cup flour

Put the squirrel in a slow cooker and add the carrots and potatoes. Cover with water. Add the celery salt, onion, garlic, and sweet basil; cook very slowly on low heat. When the squirrel starts to fall off the bone, remove and debone, making sure all the bones are removed. (Keep in mind some of the bones are very small.) Continue cooking until the meat is very tender. Thicken with sour cream and flour. Check the stew for seasoning and serve hot.

Wildcat Springs Squirrel Stew

2 squirrels, cleaned and dejointed
5 cups hot chicken stock
I teaspoon salt
$^1/_2$ teaspoon fresh ground pepper
2 onions, diced
I cup celery, diced
I cup carrots, diced
I green bell pepper, diced
2 tablespoons bacon fat
$^1/_2$ cup brown rice
3 tablespoons flour

Place the squirrels in a pressure cooker with stock, salt, and pepper. Pressure cook at 15 pounds pressure for about 30 minutes. Meanwhile, sauté the vegetables in bacon fat until they are tender.

Remove the squirrels from the cooker. Add the vegetables and rice to the broth in the cooker and pressure cook for about 8 minutes more at 15 pounds pressure. Cut the squirrel meat into small pieces, roll in flour, and add to the stew. Bring to a boil and serve after checking the stew for seasoning. Great with cornbread.

Armadillo Feed Texas Style

2 whole pheasants

7 pounds armadillo stew meat, diced into 1-inch pieces

2 stalks celery, chopped

1 head cabbage, chopped

8 onions, chopped

4 16-ounce packages frozen mixed vegetables

2 14.5-ounce cans rutabagas

2 15-ounce cans lima beans, drained

2 cups cut yellow beans, drained

2 14.5-ounce cans crushed tomatoes

1 teaspoon seasoned salt

1 teaspoon black pepper

1 tablespoon pickling spice

Boil the pheasants and armadillo in a large soup pot for about 20 minutes, or until tender. Use enough water to cover. Remove the meat and cut into bite-sized pieces. Discard fat and skin. Add celery, cabbage, and onions to stock, and boil for about 15 minutes, or until vegetables are almost tender. Add the frozen vegetable mix, rutabagas, lima beans, yellow beans, and tomatoes, and continue to cook until the soup has reached the desired thickness. Add the meat and simmer until the meat breaks apart, stirring occasionally with a wooden paddle. Salt and pepper to taste. Put dry pickling spice in a strong cloth bag and tie firmly with a string so it will not come apart. Drop the bag into the simmering soup, plunging it in and out for a short time until the soup tastes perfect. Serve hot. This soup is great for a large group of hunters.

PORCUPINE

You most likely won't see a hunters' show doing a porcupine hunt, but believe me, many hunters love to pop a cap at one when they come across them! And guess what? There's a whole lot of people out there who encourage this, particularly foresters who resent the porcupine's habit of "ringing" trees, leading to the tree's eventual death.

The porcupine is a slow mover, so even Aunt Betsy could whack one over the head in case of an emergency. I agree, one must have an acquired taste for the porcupine. However, it is not necessarily true that the meat tastes like fuel oil. I have found that the critter cleans out much like a rabbit and the hide peels off easily. The other good thing about porcupines is that they range in weight from 8 to 45 pounds! So, like Mikey always said, "Try it, you'll like it."

Porcupine Liver, Onion, and Celery Soup

3 pounds porcupine liver
Oil
2 large onions, sliced
2 large potatoes, cubed
1 10.5-ounce can of cream of celery soup
Seasoning salt and pepper

Soak the whole liver in salted water for 30 minutes. Remove, drain, and wipe dry. Cut the liver into ³/₄-inch slices. Drop the slices into boiling water for 2 minutes. Remove, drain, and cool. Remove the thin membrane from the edges and all gristle and tubes. Brown the liver in oil. Add the sliced onions, potatoes, and soup. Cover and simmer for about 45 minutes. Check for seasoning and serve hot.

Hawkeye Porcupine Tailgating Soup

Go Hawks!

6 slices bacon, diced
3 tablespoons butter
$^1/_2$ cup celery, diced
2 cups red potatoes, diced
I large onion, diced
$^1/_2$ cup carrots, diced
3 tablespoons flour
3 cups chicken stock
I teaspoon creole seasoning salt
2 cups cooked porcupine meat, diced
I cup corn kernels
2 cups half-and-half
2 cups canned tomatoes, diced
Salt and pepper to taste

Fry the bacon in a Dutch oven; remove and drain on paper towels. Add butter to the bacon drippings. Add the celery, potatoes, onions, and carrots. Sauté, stirring constantly, until the onions and celery are tender. Stir in the flour until well incorporated. Add the chicken stock and seasoning salt, stirring to blend well. Cook, stirring, until soup thickens. Cover and simmer for 15 minutes. Add the porcupine and corn; simmer for about 10 minutes. Add the half-and-half and tomatoes. Check the soup for seasoning and simmer for 20 minutes. Serve hot at your favorite college football tailgating party!

Travis (The Duke's) Porcupine Lumberjack Stew

2 pounds porcupine meat, cut into 1-inch cubes
Butter
2 diced onions
1 cup beer
$^1/_2$ cup sweet corn
$^1/_2$ cup cooked pinto beans
1 cup brown gravy
1 tablespoon brown sugar
1 teaspoon red wine
1 teaspoon garlic salt with parsley

In a cooking pot, brown the meat in butter until no longer pink. Add the remaining ingredients and simmer on low for about 8 hours, stirring every 30 minutes or so. To thicken stew, mix $^1/_4$ cup flour with water and slowly add to stew. Check the stew for seasoning and serve.

Cousin Rick Black's Hunting Dogs' Liver Soup

A great soup your dogs will love.

2 tablespoons vegetable oil
2 pounds wild game liver of your choice, trimmed of membranes and chopped fine
2 liters basic dog broth
Dash of salt
Dash of pepper
2 cups heavy cream
4 tablespoons flour
3 tablespoons chopped parsley
Kibble

Heat the oil in a saucepan. Add the chopped wild game liver and cook for about 5 minutes, stirring constantly. Add the broth, salt, and pepper, and bring to a boil. Reduce the heat, add the remaining ingredients, and simmer for 10 minutes. Use the kibble to thicken the soup. Your dogs will love this great soup and it is a great way to teach the young ones how to cook.

CHAPTER THREE

SOUPS AND STEWS USING BIG GAME

Some hunters have different opinions of what big game is. Deer, elk, moose, caribou, antelope, wild boar, bear, bison (buffalo), musk ox, wild goat, and wild sheep are just a few of the big boys I enjoy hunting and cooking. Here are a few tips on big game:

Always make a clean kill: A moose weighs 750 to 1,700 pounds. When butchered, the carcass weighs around 350 to 850 pounds, of which about 250 to 700 pounds is edible meat. With that said, the distance from camp is a major factor! Make sure, before taking down a large animal, that you can get it back to camp before the meat starts to spoil.

Don't let the flavor of your meat run away: Where the animal is and where it may run to will greatly affect the quality of the meat. A resting and calm animal just before it is killed quickly will have by far better tasting meat than an animal that is stressed or suffers a prolonged death. Running, fear, rutting, and swimming will affect the taste of your harvest.

Know your weapon and how it shoots: Shot placement and type of weapon will also affect the flavor of your meat. Always try for a quick, clean kill, which will minimize meat damage. From an early age I was taught to make a heart or lung shot. The head and neck shot are risky because they can result in the loss or wounding of game. Did you know that the brain on a caribou is about the size of a baseball and encased in bone, while the heart and lung area is about the size of a basketball? A neck shot may hit the esophagus or trachea thus allowing the animal to run off, leaving no blood trail, and dying a slow, painful death. Always make sure to have a weapon with enough power and accuracy for the game you are pursuing. If you are bowhunting, carry a large sidearm, just in case.

Be sharp when it comes to butchering your harvest: My dad had a favorite saying: "Once you pull the trigger, the fun stops and the work begins." Bleed the animal quickly. Your bullet or broad head may have done this for you or you may have to do it with your knife. Take a little time to lay out your tarp and organize your thoughts and equipment.

Pick the brain: There are many ways to gut and butcher big game, and I have learned many from books, friends, and the pros. Whichever way you choose, remember that cleanliness is the path to take. Keep in mind that you are working with food, so treat it appropriately. Always keep hair, leaves, and tundra off of it as much as possible. Have water to rinse off any rumen, bile, or urine that gets on the meat.

Tag it and bag it: Put the meat in game bags as soon as you can. Avoid those bags that look like cheesecloth; they will rip just about every time. Spend the bucks and buy the more expensive bags that look like coarse pillowcases. Bag all of your meat before you take your first load back to camp. If the big critter died in the brush, move the meat into the open, away from the carcass. I once had a bear feeding on the skin and gut pile of a kill I had several years ago. To say that I was freaked out when I walked up on him doing this would be an understatement!

Hang 'em high: When you get the meat back to camp, hang it in a tree, on a rack, or in a small stand of alders. Your hanging area or meat pole should be close enough to your camp that you can see it, but not so close that a bear could cause you problems (that's called a dumb attack). Never store your meat in plastic bags.

When your meat is back in camp, the hard part is done, but there are still some critical steps that need to be taken before it gets to the freezer. The most important thing is to keep the meat cool and dry and allow air to circulate around it.

DEER

Deer live in woodlands all over Europe, Asia, northern Africa, and America. There are many deer species of various sizes, but all the males (bucks) grow antlers. The meat (venison) is lean and has a gamey flavor that can be made milder if soaked overnight in a cooler. Because I live in Iowa, our great-tasting whitetail has spoiled me. Most of the deer in the Midwest eat corn and soybeans and do not have strong gamey-tasting meat. This is great for the hunter but tough on the poor farmer who loses thousands of hard-earned dollars a year due to deer and turkey raiding their fields.

Deer Burger Chowder

³/₄ pound deer burger

14 ounces canned tomatoes, diced

3 potatoes, sliced

1 white onion, chopped

3 garlic cloves, minced

1 green bell pepper, chopped

Salt and pepper to taste

2 tablespoons chili powder

3 tablespoons flour

In a pressure cooker, sauté the deer burger; add the tomatoes, potatoes, onion, garlic, bell pepper, and salt and pepper to taste. Mix well. Cover securely and cook on high until steam is created. Place the weight on the cover stem. When the weight begins to rock, turn the heat to medium to allow the weight to rock gently and cook for about 15 minutes. Cool the pot by passing cold water over the cover and carefully remove the weight. Open the cover after the steam has been totally vented. Make a paste from the chili powder and flour and add to the chowder. Heat on medium, uncovered, and serve hot.

Cedar Rapids Deer Barley Soup

3 pounds venison short ribs

2 tablespoons olive oil

7 cups water

16 ounces canned tomatoes

1 yellow onion, sliced

2 tablespoons beef bouillon granules

2 teaspoons salt

1 teaspoon basil

$^1/_2$ teaspoon Worcestershire sauce

2 cups carrots, sliced

1 cup celery, sliced

1 cup barley

$^1/_2$ cup green bell pepper, chopped

$^1/_4$ cup parsley

In a large kettle, brown the venison short ribs over low heat. Drain well. Stir in water, undrained tomatoes, onion, bouillon granules, salt, basil, and Worcestershire sauce. Cover and simmer for about 2 hours. Stir in carrots, celery, barley, green peppers, and parsley. Cover and simmer for about 45 minutes. Remove the venison ribs. When cool enough to handle, cut off the meat and coarsely chop, discarding the bones when done. Skim off the fat from the soup. Return the meat to the soup and heat through. Season to taste with salt and pepper and serve hot.

Camp Trigger-Happy Venison and Lentil Stew

1 pound deer burger
$1/2$ cup white onion, chopped
1 garlic clove, minced
4 ounces canned mushrooms, stems and pieces
16 ounces canned tomatoes
1 celery stalk, chopped
1 carrot, sliced
1 cup lentils, uncooked
3 cups water
$1/4$ cup red wine
1 bay leaf
2 tablespoons parsley, snipped
1 teaspoon salt
1 teaspoon instant beef bouillon
$1/2$ teaspoon pepper

Cook and stir the deer burger, onion, and garlic in a Dutch oven until the deer burger is brown with no pink showing. Drain off the excess fat and stir in the undrained mushrooms and the remaining ingredients. Heat the stew to boiling; reduce heat, cover, and simmer, stirring occasionally, until the lentils are tender, about 45 minutes. Remove the bay leaf, check for seasoning, and serve hot.

Betsy Lou's Caribou Stew

4 tablespoons bacon drippings
5 onions, coarsely chopped
2 green bell peppers, chopped
3 garlic cloves, minced
2 tablespoons paprika
3 pounds caribou stew meat, cubed
Seasoning salt and pepper to taste
6 ounces tomato paste
1 cup sour cream and chives, at cabin temperature
   (room temperature)

Preheat the oven to 325 degrees. Heat the bacon fat in a deep, heavy pot and cook the onions, peppers, and garlic until all is tender and the onions are transparent. Add the paprika, caribou stew meat, and the remaining ingredients except for the cup of sour cream and chives. Stir well. Simmer in preheated oven for about 2 hours, or until the meat is tender. Adjust the oven temperature during cooking time so the contents of the pot remain at a slow simmer. Serve Betsy Lou's Caribou Stew in shallow soup bowls with a tablespoon of sour cream and chives atop each serving.

Old Man Black's Elk Meat Soup

I pound elk roast meat with bone
2 bay leaves
4 juniper berries
2 cloves
Bacon fat for browning
8 cups beef stock
$^1/_2$ cup white wine
I tablespoon Worcestershire sauce
4 red potatoes, quartered
I carrot, peeled and sliced
I parsnip, peeled and diced
$^1/_2$ cup cabbage, shredded
2 celery ribs, chopped
2 banana peppers, chopped
$^1/_2$ cup green peas

Trim the elk meat from the bone and cube in coarse pieces. Simmer the bone in water with bay leaves, juniper, and cloves for about 2 hours. Remove the bone and strain the stock. Return the broth to the pot. In a large skillet, brown the meat in bacon fat. Add to the pot. Add the remaining ingredients except the peas and simmer for another 45 minutes. Add the peas just minutes before serving.

Yarlem Ranch Hunters Soup

I cup kidney beans
I cup pinto beans
2 pounds elk meat, cubed
I cup white onions, coarsely chopped
I cup celery, coarsely chopped
$^1/_4$ cup carrots, coarsely chopped
I teaspoon garlic, minced
3 quarts beef stock
$^1/_4$ teaspoon Tabasco
Salt and pepper to taste
$^1/_4$ cup tomato paste

Soak the beans in cold water overnight. Rinse; drain until dry. Heat oil in a soup pot, and brown the elk meat. Add the onions, celery, carrots, and garlic; sauté until tender. Add the beef stock and beans. Simmer for about 60 minutes, or until the beans are tender. Add the Tabasco, salt, and pepper. Stir in the tomato paste, simmer for about 15 minutes, and serve hot.

Roaming Buffalo Steak and Bean Chowder

I pound boneless bison sirloin steak, cut in $^1/_2$-inch cubes
I medium onion, chopped
2 14.5-ounce cans whole tomatoes, undrained and chopped
I 15-ounce can spicy chili beans, undrained
2 baking potatoes, unpeeled, cut into $^1/_2$-inch cubes
$^1/_2$ teaspoon cumin

Spray a nonstick Dutch oven with nonstick cooking spray. Heat over medium-high heat until hot. Add the bison meat; cook and stir until no longer pink. Add the onions; cook for 2 minutes, stirring constantly. Add all the remaining ingredients and bring to a boil. Reduce the heat to medium-low; partially cover and simmer for about 30 minutes, or until the potatoes are tender. Check the chowder for seasoning and serve.

BISON (BUFFALO)

Tips from Cousin Rick and his friends at Quarry Creek Elk & Bison:
Buffalo is native to North America. Once about sixty million in number, bison were hunted almost to extinction by the 1890s. More than
280,000 buffalo are being raised across North America today. I'm
from Iowa, and the best tasting buffalo meat in my neck of the
woods is from Quarry Creek Elk & Bison in Fort Madison, Iowa. I
asked the gang there for a few tips on cooking buffalo meat, which
is rich in flavor and is believed to be an all-natural cancer-fighting
food. They have found that buffalo meat is similar to beef and can
be cooked in much the same way. The taste is often indistinguish-
able from beef, although bison tends to have a fuller, sweeter flavor.
It is not gamey or wild tasting. Bison is very low in fat and cholesterol
and is high in protein, vitamins, and minerals. When cooking buffalo, especially the steaks and roasts, it is better to marinate them.
Marinades and seasonings enhance the taste and texture of the
meat. Quarry Creek says that buffalo meat is lean, and they recommend cooking your buffalo soups and stews in a Dutch oven or
crock. If it sounds like your old Cousin Rick is a big fan of buffalo, I
am! They are a blast to hunt and make for great-tasting soups and
stews. And if you can't hunt them, visit the great team at www.
quarrycreek.com and tell them old cousin Rick said hey.

Worthington Oven Bison Stew

$^1/_4$ cup all-purpose flour

2 pounds bison stew meat, cubed

2 tablespoons vegetable oil

1 14.5-ounce can stewed tomatoes

5 carrots, chopped

3 potatoes, peeled and cubed

1 cup frozen peas

1 cup beer

1-ounce package dry onion soup mix

1 tablespoon soy sauce

1 teaspoon garlic salt

$^1/_2$ teaspoon ground black pepper

Preheat the oven to 400 degrees. Place the flour in a large resealable plastic bag. Pour in the meat, seal the bag, and shake well to coat. Spread the oil in the bottom of a roasting pan, and then arrange the bison meat in a single layer in the pan. Bake the meat at 400 degrees for about 40 minutes. Remove it from the oven and add the remaining ingredients. Stir with a wooden spoon, cover, and return stew to the oven. Reduce the temperature to 375 degrees and bake for another 2 hours. Check for seasoning and serve hot.

COUSIN RICK LIVED TO TELL THE STORY!

The first time old Cousin Rick booked a hunt with an experienced outfitter, he knew he would be deer hunting a productive area filled with deer and grizzly bears. When he got to camp, he insisted that his guide be 60 years old or older. Now the outfitter thought this was odd, because at the time old Cousin Rick was in his early twenties. Well, Cousin Rick downed a very nice buck, but skinning and butchering the deer attracted some big grizzlies. So when Cousin Rick returned to base camp with his clothes shredded, telling the story of being attacked by a bear, the outfitter wanted to know where his old guide was. Cousin Rick said he was still laying in the woods. The outfitter asked him how his clothes got torn, and Rick said that while they were working on the deer carcass, a grizzly ambushed them and he was attacked. Rick said, "I hit the bear with my gun and took off running. As I was running away the old guide yelled to me that you couldn't outrun a bear. I yelled back, 'I don't have to outrun the bear, I just have to outrun you!'"

Smoky Mountain Bear and Cabbage Soup

I pound ground bear meat
$^1/_2$ teaspoon garlic salt
$^1/_4$ teaspoon garlic powder
$^1/_4$ teaspoon black pepper
2 ribs celery, chopped
16 ounces canned kidney beans, drained
$^1/_2$ head cabbage, chopped
28 ounces canned tomatoes, chopped
I small white onion, diced
2 cups beef stock
Chopped parsley

In a Dutch oven, brown the bear meat until it is no longer pink. Add the remaining ingredients except the parsley; bring to a boil. Reduce the heat and simmer, covered, for about 60 minutes. Garnish with parsley and serve.

Sarasota County Game Soup

This is one of my most requested wild game feed soups.

I pound ground boar
I pound ground wild goat
I pound ground venison
$^1/_2$ gallon chicken stock
$^1/_2$ gallon beef stock
I ounce Worcestershire sauce
I cup diced tomatoes
I diced onion
I diced stalk celery
I diced green bell pepper
2 diced carrots
$^1/_2$ cup peas
$^1/_2$ cup okra
$^1/_4$ cup lima beans
$^1/_2$ cup sweet corn
2 teaspoons minced garlic
Salt and pepper to taste

Combine all the ingredients in a large soup kettle and bring to a boil. Reduce the heat and simmer for about 4 hours, skimming fat off the top as needed. Check the soup for seasoning and serve hot. *Note:* I have also used $^1/_4$ cup diced banana peppers and 1 diced jalapeño pepper for more flavor.

Saber-Tooth Wild Boar Soup

1 15-ounce can cream-style corn
1 cup milk
1 cup diced wild boar meat
$^1/_2$ teaspoon sweet basil
$^1/_2$ teaspoon cilantro
$^1/_2$ teaspoon steak seasoning
1 teaspoon hot curry powder
1 roasted Ortega chile, minced
$^1/_4$ teaspoon dried minced onions
$^1/_4$ teaspoon garlic salt
$^1/_4$ teaspoon seasoned salt
$^1/_4$ teaspoon 5-spice

Put all the ingredients together in a large saucepan and heat thoroughly over medium heat. Serve in warm bowls garnished with lime wedges.

Apapaho Hunting Club Beer And Antelope Stew

4 pounds antelope blade steaks, I inch thick, trimmed of fat, diced
Salt and black pepper to taste
3 tablespoons olive oil
8 cups yellow onions, chopped
I tablespoon tomato paste
2 teaspoons minced garlic
3 tablespoons flour
I cup chicken stock
I cup beef stock
I cup dark ale
3 sprigs fresh thyme, tied with kitchen twine
2 bay leaves
I tablespoons cider vinegar

Dry the antelope meat thoroughly with paper towels, and then season generously with salt and pepper. On the stovetop, heat 2 teaspoons olive oil in a large Dutch oven until the oil begins to smoke; add a third of the antelope meat to the pot. Cook, without moving the pieces, until well browned; using tongs, turn each piece and continue cooking until the second side is well browned. Transfer the cooked meat to a separate bowl. Repeat with second third of meat and an additional 2 teaspoons olive oil. When all the meat is cooked, add 1 tablespoon olive oil to Dutch oven. Add the onions and tomato paste and cook, scraping the bottom of the pot with a wooden spoon, until the onions are tender. Add all the remaining ingredients, including the cooked antelope meat, and simmer on low heat for about 4 hours, stirring at least every 10 minutes. Discard thyme and bay leaves. Adjust the seasonings with salt and pepper and serve hot. (I serve this stew over fried potatoes at our camp.)

Cousin Rick's Musk Ox Stew with Almonds and Apricots

I teaspoon ground ginger

I teaspoon ground black pepper

I teaspoon cinnamon

$^1/_4$ teaspoon turmeric

$^1/_4$ teaspoon cayenne

$^1/_4$ teaspoon ground coriander

$^1/_4$ teaspoon cardamom

$^1/_4$ teaspoon nutmeg

$^1/_4$ teaspoon cloves

$^1/_2$ cup beer

3 pounds musk ox neck roast, trimmed of fat and cut into 2-inch cubes

$^1/_2$ cup unsalted butter

2 chopped white onions

2 chopped garlic cloves

2 cinnamon sticks

3 cups chicken stock

2 cups roughly chopped apricots

2 cups almonds, whole and blanched

$^1/_3$ cup honey

I cup carrots, cut into $^1/_2$-inch-thick slices

2 teaspoons lemon juice

$^1/_2$ cup flat-leaf parsley, chopped

In a large bowl, combine the ginger, pepper, cinnamon, turmeric, cayenne, coriander, cardamom, nutmeg, cloves, and beer. Mix well. Add the ox meat and rub in the paste, coating evenly. Cover and refrigerate for 6 hours, or overnight. In a Dutch oven or heavy, lidded pot, melt the butter. Add the onions, garlic, and cinnamon sticks, and simmer until the onions are tender and the mixture is fragrant. Add the marinated meat, including the marinade, and then the chicken stock to the pot. Bring the stock to a boil and skim off any froth that appears. Reduce the heat to low, cover, and simmer, stirring from time to time. Add beer if the pot becomes too dry. Stew until the meat is tender, about 2 hours, more if needed. Add the apricots, almonds, honey, and carrots, and simmer, uncovered, stirring often to prevent scorching, until the meat is very soft and almost falling apart, about 30 minutes longer. The sauce should reduce to a syrupy glaze. At this point, taste it and add the lemon juice as desired. Let the stew cool for 24 hours in the cooler. Stir in the chopped parsley, check for seasoning, and warm well before serving.

Buffalo Bouillon Soup

4 pounds buffalo tail, patted dry
Salt and pepper
2 onions, peeled and quartered
2 carrots, cut into 1-inch slices
Zest of 1 orange, removed in strips with a vegetable peeler
1 cup dry white wine
4 quarts water
$1/3$ cup fresh cranberries
12 ounces mushrooms, chopped coarse
3 ribs celery, cut into 1-inch slices
4 sprigs of thyme
1 bay leaf
4 cloves
1 teaspoon peppercorns

Preheat the oven to 450 degrees. In a large roasting pan, combine the buffalo tail (patted dry and seasoned with salt and pepper), onions, carrots, and orange zest. Roast the mixture in the middle of the oven, turning the tail until brown, and then transfer to a large stockpot. Deglaze the roasting pan with the wine over high heat, scraping the brown bits, and add the deglazing liquid to the stockpot with water, cranberries, mushrooms, celery, thyme, bay leaf, cloves, and peppercorns. Bring the liquid to a boil, skimming the froth, and simmer gently, uncovered, for about 4 hours. Ladle the mixture through a sieve lined with a rinsed and squeezed kitchen towel into a large bowl. Reserve the buffalo tail for another use. Discard the remaining solids. This bouillon can be made 3 days in advance and kept chilled. Discard excess fat (leave enough to cover soup when chilled). Bring the buffalo bouillon just to a boil and ladle it into warmed bowls.

Custer's Last Stand Soup

2 tablespoons olive oil
I large chopped onion
I minced garlic clove
$^1/_2$ cup tomato sauce
3 quarts beef stock
2 sliced carrots
$^1/_2$ pound string beans, chopped into I-inch slices
$^1/_3$ cup uncooked rice
I pound ground elk
$^1/_2$ cup chopped parsley
I teaspoon salt
$^1/_2$ teaspoon fresh ground black pepper
I egg
2 cups fresh peas
I teaspoon oregano
$^1/_2$ cup chopped cilantro

Heat the oil in a heavy cast saucepan. Add the onion and minced garlic, and sauté until all is tender, about 5 minutes or so. Add the tomato sauce and beef stock. Bring to a boil and simmer. Add the carrots and string beans. Prepare meatballs by mixing the rice into the ground elk and adding the parsley, salt, and pepper. Add the egg and form elk meat into 1-inch elk balls. Return the soup to a gentle simmer. Add the elk balls to the soup, cover, and let simmer for about 40 minutes. Add the peas during the last 15 minutes of cooking. Add the oregano and sprinkle with salt and pepper to taste. Garnish the soup with fresh cilantro.

ANTELOPE

Antelope meat is leaner, but similar in taste to that of deer. The males are called bucks, bulls, or stags; females, does or cows; and unweaned young are fawns or calves. Some of the best-tasting antelope I have cooked with was farm raised. Although rigorous, antelope hunting is truly a sport I enjoy.

Uncle Marvin and Cousin Rick were driving through the county to go bear hunting. They came upon a fork in the road where a county sign read "Bear Left" so they went home.

Skip Dover's Spicy Wild Sheep Stew

3 pounds wild sheep stew meat, cubed
Olive oil
1 cup white wine
2 chopped onions
4 minced garlic cloves
2 red bell peppers, chopped
2 dry pasilla chiles, chopped, stems and most seeds removed
1 tablespoon hot paprika
1 teaspoon cumin
$1/4$ teaspoon cardamom
2 cups chicken stock
14 ounces tomato paste
10 sprigs fresh leaf parsley
5 sprigs thyme
1 bay leaf
$1/3$ cup golden raisins
$1/3$ cup currants
Seasoned salt and pepper to taste

Heat a tablespoon of olive oil in a large, heavy, high-sided skillet over medium-high heat. When the skillet is hot, add the wild sheep meat pieces in batches, being careful not to crowd them. Cook, turning as needed, so the meat browns evenly on all sides. Transfer to a bowl. Pour excess oil over the meat. Return the skillet to medium high heat and add the wine, stirring with a wooden spoon to release any meat bits that have stuck to the pan. Cook for about 3 minutes and pour the mixture over the wild sheep meat. Return the skillet to medium-high heat and add a tablespoon of olive oil. Add the onions and garlic, cover, and cook for about 5 minutes, or until tender. Add the bell peppers and pasilla chiles and cook, uncovered, for about 20 minutes.

Transfer all ingredients, including all cooked ingredients, to a stockpot and simmer for about 3 hours, turning every 5 minutes or so. Season with seasoned salt and pepper and serve hot.

Casper Capp's Wild Boar and White Bean Soup

1 pound Northern white beans
3 pounds smoked wild boar shanks (each shank cut into 3 sections)
2 quarts chicken stock
1 cup diced onions
1 cup chopped celery
2/3 cup chopped carrots
2 diced garlic cloves
Tabasco sauce
Garlic salt and pepper
Herbes de Provence
Fresh parsley

Soak the beans in at least 2 quarts of cold water for about 4 hours. Drain the water. Put the wild boar shanks pieces in a large pot and cover with chicken stock. Bring to a simmer for about 60 minutes. Add the chopped vegetables and beans. Cook for another 60 minutes, until the vegetables are soft and the boar meat easily pulls away from the bone. Add several drops of Tabasco and the garlic salt and pepper to taste. Add a pinch of herbes de Provence. Serve hot with a pinch of chopped fresh parsley.

Buck-in-Rut Baked Venison and Vegetable Soup

I make this soup a couple of days before deer camp.

4 pounds venison short ribs
I onion, skin on
3 garlic cloves, peeled and crushed
4 whole peppercorns
4 cups beef broth
3 leeks, trimmed and julienned with I-inch of green remaining
3 carrots, julienned
3 celery ribs, julienned
8 white mushroom caps, sliced
2 cups shaped pasta, cooked until just tender
Salt and fresh black pepper to taste
2 tablespoons chopped dill
2 tablespoons parsley

Preheat the oven to 350 degrees. Place the venison, onion, garlic, peppercorns, and broth in an ovenproof casserole. Add water to cover. Bring to a boil. Cover and bake for about 2 hours, until the venison is very tender. Remove the venison and cool. Shred the meat from the bones, discarding any fat and the bones. Pour the broth through a fine mesh strainer into a bowl. Allow to cool. Pour or skim off fat and return this broth to the casserole. Add leeks, carrots, and celery to the casserole. Bring to a boil; reduce heat and simmer, covered, for about 3 minutes. Add the shredded venison to the broth with the mushrooms, pasta, salt, and pepper. Bake, covered, for about 5 minutes. Remove the soup from the oven and stir in the dill and parsley. Serve hot after checking for seasoning.

Gem Creek Venison Soup Stock

3 pounds bone and venison meat

2 tablespoons fat

$^1/_2$ cup chopped celery

$^1/_2$ cup chopped white onions

5 whole cloves

2 sprigs of parsley

3 quarts water

$^1/_2$ cup chopped carrots

I teaspoon salt

$^1/_2$ teaspoon thyme

$^1/_2$ teaspoon marjoram

2 bay leaves

Cut the meat from the bones and brown well in fat. Cover the bones and browned meat with water. Add the remaining ingredients, cover, and simmer for about 4 hours. Strain, chill, remove fat, and strain again.

COUSIN RICK'S TIPS FOR FREEZING YOUR HARVEST

- Trim the fat to reduce the strong flavor changes that may occur during freezer storage.
- Divide the meat into meal-sized quantities.
- To prevent freezer burn, use moisture- or vapor-proof wrap, such as heavily waxed freezer wrap, laminated freezer wrap, heavy-duty aluminum foil, or plastic freezer storage bags. Speaking from experience, I advise you to not use garbage bags.
- Press all of the air out before sealing.
- Label packages with the contents and the date.
- Freeze only the amount of meat that will become solidly frozen within 24 hours.
- Avoid overloading the freezer. (I have my own wild game freezer in my garage).
- Space packages in freezer to allow air to circulate for quick cooling and freezing.

Archer's Caribou Camp Stew

I pound caribou, cut in cubes
2 tablespoons flour
2 tablespoons butter
3 cups boiling water
I cup pearl onions
1/2 clove garlic
I teaspoons salt
1/2 teaspoon paprika
I teaspoon sugar
I tablespoon dry white wine
I tablespoon Worcestershire sauce
1/2 cup tomato juice
1/2 cup sliced carrots
2 tablespoons minced onions
1/2 cup diced celery
I cup cubed red potatoes

Flour the meat and brown it in butter in a heavy pan. Add the boiling water, pearl onions, garlic, salt, paprika, sugar, wine, Worcestershire sauce, and tomato juice. Cover tightly and simmer for about 2 hours, adding more water if needed. Add the remaining ingredients and continue cooking until the vegetables are tender. To thicken stew, add a flour-and-water paste. Check for seasoning and serve hot.

Arkansas Andy's Wild Boar and Hominy Soup

I pound ground boar
I white onion, diced
4 cloves garlic, crushed
I teaspoon crushed chiltepin
10 cups cooked hominy
7 cups chicken stock
46 ounces canned tomatoes, chopped
Juice of 3 limes
Salt and pepper to taste

Place the ground boar meat, onion, garlic, and chiltepin in a large skillet or Dutch oven and gently cook until the onion is transparent and the boar meat is cooked through. Drain off any fat. Add the remaining ingredients and simmer for 2 hours, stirring often. Check the soup for seasoning before serving.

Sergeant Slaughter's BBQ Boar and Cream Soup

Butter
1 pound cubed boar meat, cooked
1 pound wild boar meat, barbecued and sliced in strips
Flour
1 teaspoon white pepper
2 teaspoons Worcestershire sauce
1 teaspoon Louisiana hot sauce
2 teaspoons garlic salt with parsley
2 cups chicken stock
1 quart milk
4 tablespoons Madeira
$^1/_2$ cup chopped green onions

Melt about 2 tablespoons butter in a large saucepan over low heat. Add the cubed and barbecued boar meat and mix together. Add about 2 tablespoons flour and stir constantly for about 5 minutes, not allowing mixture to burn. Add all the seasonings to the chicken stock and slowly add the stock to the meat mixture. Slowly add the milk and stir until well blended. Let the soup simmer for about 30 minutes, stirring constantly. Just before serving stir in the Madeira. Check the soup for seasoning and serve hot. *Note:* This is a very touchy soup to cook. Take your time and adjust the seasonings to your taste. When mastered, this will be one of your most-used wild boar soup recipes!

Seven-Millimeter Moose Stew

2 tablespoons olive oil
2 pounds moose stew meat, cubed
2 small sliced onions
2 sliced celery stalks
2 teaspoons seasoned salt
1 teaspoon white pepper
1 bay leaf
1 teaspoon marjoram
1 teaspoon garlic powder
1 teaspoon sweet basil
2 sliced carrots
1 32-ounce can tomatoes
2 cups frozen sweet corn
2 cups frozen green beans
1 cup butter beans
4 potatoes, cubed
4 cups beef stock
1 cup dark beer
1 cup lite beer

In a Dutch oven or large kettle, heat oil just to smoking; add the meat and brown rapidly until all is browned. Reduce the heat and add the onions, celery, and spices. Simmer until the onions are tender. Add the remaining ingredients and cook over medium heat until the meat is tender. Check the soup for seasoning and serve hot.

CARIBOU

Caribou or reindeer are slightly larger than white-tailed deer. Both males and females have antlers (racks). The meat is somewhat sweeter than other venison. Caribou live primarily in North America and Siberia. Although I have not had the chance to hunt caribou, I have been lucky enough to have several hundred pounds of fresh caribou meat given to me by hunting buddies. It is great-tasting venison!

Quarry Creek Elk and Bison Company Elk and Bison Soup

The best tasting elk in Fort Madison, Iowa!

1 pound elk meat, cubed
1 pound bison meat, cubed
8 cups beef stock
2 bay leaves
1 teaspoon juniper
1 clove, chopped
Bacon fat
$^1/_2$ cup white wine
1 tablespoon Worcestershire sauce
4 small potatoes, quartered
1 carrot, peeled and sliced
1 parsnip, peeled and diced
$^1/_2$ cup turnip, peeled and diced
$^1/_2$ cup cabbage, shredded
2 celery ribs, chopped
2 banana peppers, chopped
$^1/_2$ cup green peas

If the meat has bones, trim the meat from the bones and cube coarsely. Simmer the bones in beef stock with bay leaves, juniper, and cloves for about 2 hours. Remove the bones and strain the stock. Return the broth to the pot. In a large skillet, brown the meat in bacon fat and add it to the pot. Add the remaining ingredients except the peas and simmer for about 30 minutes. Add the peas just before serving. This is a great soup to make before camp and is very good reheated the next day.

Doc Anderson's Elk Soup

2 pounds elk meat
$^1/_2$ pound elk bones, with good marrow
10 cups beef stock
I tablespoon salt
2 tablespoons butter
$^1/_2$ pound elk liver, sliced into cubes
2 carrots, unpeeled and chopped
2 stalks celery, chopped
I large onion, chopped
I turnip, peeled and diced
Salt to taste
I bay leaf
I teaspoon black peppercorns
$^1/_4$ teaspoon saffron
I cup cold water
Eggs

Rinse the elk meat and bones and place them in a large pot with the beef stock. Bring to a simmer very slowly. Do not skim the brown foam, it will eventually sink and strengthen the broth. In the meantime, melt the butter in a pan and stir in the elk liver and vegetables, frying until they are golden brown. Stir the salt into the broth; then scrape in the liver and vegetables, and rinse the frying pan with broth into the soup. Add the remaining ingredients except eggs. Simmer on low heat for about 3 hours. While the soup is cooking, skim away all fat. Heat the soup to a full boil just before serving. Ladle the hot soup into small bowls and break open 1 raw egg into each bowl of soup.

Wild Boar Balls Soup

6 cups chicken stock
**I cup cellophane noodles, soaked in cold water for 20 minutes,
then cut into 6-inch lengths**
^{1}/$_2$ cup smoked ham, finely chopped
^{1}/$_2$ cup wild boar meat, ground
2 tablespoons water chestnuts, minced
^{1}/$_2$ teaspoon cornstarch
I tablespoon soy sauce
2 tablespoons green onions, minced

Boil the stock in a large saucepan and stir in the soaked cellophane noodles. Reduce the heat and simmer for about 20 minutes.
Meanwhile, mix together the chopped ham, ground boar meat, and
water chestnuts with the cornstarch and soy sauce. Shape the meat
into little balls and drop them into the soup. Continue cooking for
about 20 more minutes. Check the soup for seasoning and serve in
bowls garnished with the minced green onions.

Flatheads Basic Boar Soup

^{1}/$_2$ pound wild boar shoulder
I onion
6 cups vegetable stock
^{1}/$_4$ pound fresh mushrooms, sliced
I teaspoon salt
^{1}/$_4$ teaspoon white pepper
I cup peas

Cut the boar shoulder in 1-inch cubes and the onion in quarters.
Place in a heavy pan with stock and mushrooms and bring slowly to
a boil. Reduce the heat, and skim surface clear. Then simmer, covered, for about 2 hours. Stir in salt and pepper and simmer for
another 5 minutes. During the last 20 minutes of cooking, stir in the
peas. Serve hot after rechecking seasoning.

Corley's Antelope Cheese Ball Soup

1 pound ground antelope
1 tablespoon butter
1 white onion, chopped
1 clove garlic, minced
1 28-ounce can whole tomatoes, mashed
18 ounces tomato juice
15 ounces tomato sauce
15 ounces canned pinto beans
1 tablespoon Worcestershire sauce
1 teaspoon basil
$^{1}/_{2}$ teaspoon pepper
2 eggs
$^{1}/_{2}$ cup grated Parmesan cheese
$^{1}/_{2}$ teaspoon thyme leaves
$^{1}/_{2}$ cup finely rolled cracker crumbs
4 cups shredded cabbage

Brown the meat in butter and set aside to cool. Place the onion, garlic, tomatoes, tomato juice, tomato sauce, beans, Worcester sauce, basil, and pepper in a large kettle. Bring mixture to a boil, cover, and simmer for about 45 minutes. Combine the eggs, Parmesan, thyme, crackers, and browned antelope meat. Mix well and shape into 1-inch balls. When the soup has simmered for 45 minutes, stir in the cabbage and drop in the meatballs. Cover and simmer for another 45 minutes and serve hot.

COUSIN RICK SAYS "HERE'S WHAT YOU NEED TO KNOW TO PICK OUT A GREAT SOUP POT"

Yeah, buddy, buying a good soup pot, also what I call a cook's pot, is important to every outdoor cook because of its versatility. Not only do I use it for making my delicious wild game soups, stews, and chilies, it comes in pretty darn handy when I cook pasta, make stocks, braise meats, make my famous homemade tomato sauce, and plenty more. So I'm tellin' you to buy something that will work well for every type of cookin' you do and one that will hold up for many years to come. Here are some things to look at when choosing a good soup pot:

Size matters: Soup pots typically come in sizes ranging as small as 4 quart to as large as 20 quart, before getting into commercial sizes like I use for game feeds. I have found that a soup pot doesn't have to be as big as a stock pot because you typically don't make as big a batch. You don't need to have one pot for soup and another one for stock. For the average wild game cook I recommend you look in the 6-quart to 12-quart range so your pot will be versatile enough for your other cooking needs.

The shape of things: A soup pot usually has a round base, deep straight sides, and a cover. Although this shape is more important when making stocks and stock reductions, it works well for making soups too. Could you use a shorter, smaller, wider pan for making wild game soups? Heck yeah, and depending on how much you are making, you just may want to use a large saucepan instead. I have even used a turkey fry pot for soups at camp.

Stick with thick: No matter what type of pan you buy, you want it to have a thick, heavy bottom to prevent burning. This is especially true with soup pots. All soups, including wild game ones, require time to cook, so the pan will be sitting on the stovetop for long periods. Speaking from experience, you don't want the ingredients to scorch and stick to the bottom because it is too thin or made of cheap materials. This is just a waste of time and hard-earned wild game vittles!

Fancy word—*conductivity*: What this means is the pot's ability to transmit heat from the heat source to the food and do so both evenly and efficiently. (Who knew an old country hick could get so smart?) Well-made soup pots are considered highly conductive: They can transfer heat evenly across the bottom and up the side so the food cooks the way it is supposed to. You want the soup at the bottom of the pan to be cooking evenly with the soup at the top. Every metal conducts heat differently so that's why it's important to find the right match for the type of pot you are using and the way you cook. Ever watch the old cowboy movies where the cookie in the chuck wagon had all the different pots banging around during the cattle drives?

Get a handle on it: Whether you are using it to make a great venison soup or just to boil some sweet corn, you want a well-constructed pot with a handle that you feel secure won't fall off when you are lifting a pot of hot liquid. So look for soup pots with handles that are securely attached to the pot. I recommend picking a pot that uses heavy screws or rivets with the handles. Some of the new cookware in large sporting good stores have handles that resist getting hot on your stovetop. This is great if you want to move the pot from the burner to the cabin sink, but be careful if you put it in the oven. Cool-resistant doesn't mean cool-proof. I use a good pair of silicone oven mitts when taking any cookware out of a hot oven. (Keeps my trigger finger in good shape.) Another thing to look for in a handle is the space and size. You want enough room to be able to grab with potholders and a comfortable shape for picking up.

Cousin Rick's Black Cloud Venison Soup

^{1}/2 cup corn oil
1 pound chorizo sausage, chopped
2 pounds venison rump roast, cubed
1 teaspoon salt
3 white onions, chopped
4 roasted garlic cloves, diced
1 tablespoon celery seeds
6 cups beef stock
2 cups black turtle beans, cooked
2 cups canned tomatoes, chopped
2 bay leaves
1 ancho pepper, roasted and chopped
2 tablespoons cumin
1 tablespoon chili powder
^{1}/2 tablespoon ground black pepper
2 tablespoons oregano

Heat the oil in a large skillet and add the sausage, cooking and stirring quickly to sear in the juices. Spoon the cooked chorizo over to one edge of the skillet, and add the venison cubes, stirring and cooking quickly. Add half of the salt to the cooking meat, stir well, and spoon to one side. Add the onions, garlic, and celery seeds. Cook thoroughly, stirring well. Cover and set aside. Place the stock, beans, tomatoes, and bay leaves in a large soup pot, and cook for about 30 minutes, covered, stirring occasionally. Add the hot meat mixture to the vegetable and bean pot, stirring thoroughly. Add the remaining ingredients, blending carefully, and simmer for about 30 minutes. Check the soup for seasoning and serve hot.

Heart of the Moose Soup

1 quart beef stock
1 teaspoon garlic salt
1 teaspoon pepper
1 teaspoon cider vinegar
1 large onion, chopped
4 moose marrow bones
3 tablespoons barley
2 pounds moose heart, cubed
1 head of cabbage, chopped
3 carrots, sliced
1 cup stewed tomatoes, chopped
2 teaspoons red pepper flakes
1 garlic clove, minced
1 tablespoon Frank's Red Hot Sauce
2 potatoes, diced
^{1}/2 cup beets, chopped

Place the beef stock in a large heavy pot and bring to a slow boil. Add the salt, pepper, vinegar, onions, marrow bones, and barley. Cook for about 20 minutes; then add the remaining ingredients. Cover and simmer on low heat for about 90 minutes, stirring every 10 minutes. Check the soup for seasoning and serve hot. (I recently made this soup and fried the moose heart in bacon fat first—very good!)

Wild Sheep Hunters Stew

3 potatoes, peeled and cut into $^1/_2$-inch cubes
2 pounds sauerkraut, rinsed and drained
1 onion, halved and thinly sliced
$^1/_4$ cup dry white wine
2 tablespoons cornstarch
2 cups canned diced tomatoes
$^1/_2$ teaspoon garlic powder
$^1/_2$ teaspoon pepper
$^1/_2$ teaspoon seasoning salt
2 teaspoons caraway seeds
2 pounds lean wild sheep steak, trimmed of fat and cut into cubes

Put the potatoes in a slow cooker. Top with the drained sauer-kraut and then the sliced onion. In a bowl, blend the wine and corn-starch until smooth. Stir in the diced tomatoes with juice, garlic pow-der, pepper, salt, and caraway seeds. Pour about $^2/_3$ of the tomato mixture over the potatoes and sauerkraut. Top with wild sheep meat. Pour the remaining $^1/_3$ of the tomato mixture over all. Cover and cook on low heat for about 9 hours, or until the sheep meat and potatoes are tender. Add liquid such as beer if necessary. Check the soup for seasoning before serving.

Cold Falls Basic Elk Stew

2 pounds elk roast, cut into cubes
1 pound small white onions, diced
1 pound potatoes, peeled and quartered
4 ribs celery, diced
6 carrots, sliced
2 14.5-ounce cans tomatoes, diced, drain and reserve the juice
5 tablespoons instant tapioca
1 tablespoon brown sugar
2 teaspoons Kitchen Bouquet browning sauce
1 bay leaf

Season the elk with salt and pepper. Place in a large slow cooker. Add the vegetables. Mix the tapioca, sugar, tomato liquid, and Kitchen Bouquet. Pour over stew and mix well. Add the bay leaf. Cook on low heat for about 12 hours or on high for about 6 hours. I always let the stew sit a bit before serving so it thickens a little.

Scruffy Smith's Leftover Bear Meat Soup

2 white onions, cut into small wedges

2 stalks celery, chopped

2 cups fresh mushrooms

3 garlic cloves, minced

2 tablespoons butter

2 pounds cooked bear roast, chopped

64 ounces beef broth

1 tablespoon Worcestershire sauce

Salt and pepper to taste

8 ounces uncooked egg noodles

In a large pot, cook the onions, celery, mushrooms, and garlic in butter until the onions are golden and tender. Stir in the chopped cooked bear meat. Add the beef broth and Worcestershire sauce, stirring to mix and seasoning to taste with salt and pepper. Bring mixture to a boil and then stir in the egg noodles. Reduce the heat and cook, stirring occasionally, for about 12 minutes, or until the noodles are tender.

Quixote Buffalo Sausage and White Bean Soup

2 tablespoons olive oil

2 pounds smoked buffalo sausage, sliced into bite-sized pieces

4 green onions, thinly sliced

$^3/_8$ teaspoon garlic powder

3 tomatoes, coarsely chopped

I large bell pepper, diced

I 48-ounce can white kidney beans, undrained

$^1/_4$ teaspoon black pepper

$^1/_2$ cup fresh cilantro, chopped

Water

In a large saucepan, heat the oil and cook the buffalo sausage and onion until tender. Stir in the garlic powder, tomato, and bell pepper, and cook for about 2 minutes. Stir in the beans and black pepper. Add water to cover and simmer until heated through. Stir in the cilantro right before serving.

ELK HUNTER FROM THE CITY

An elk hunter from the big city bagged a big one. Just about that time, the fish cop arrived and asked the hunter if he had a hunting license and elk tag. The hunter said he didn't have a license or a tag, so the fish cop had to take the hunter and the elk to town. The fish cop helped the hunter drag the monster elk out to the road. Now that the hard work was done, the hunter exclaimed, "I just remembered, I do have a hunting license and elk tag after all."

Jabberwocky Musk Ox and Carrot Soup

1 pound ground musk ox, browned and drained
$^1/_2$ cup onions, chopped
3 cups carrots, grated
2 10-ounce cans cream of celery soup
$^1/_2$ teaspoon garlic salt
1 teaspoon sugar
$^1/_2$ cup celery, chopped
32 ounces spicy vegetable juice
1 cup beer
$^1/_2$ teaspoon dried marjoram
$^1/_2$ teaspoon seasoned salt

Combine all in a large Dutch oven. Bring to a boil, reduce the heat and simmer, uncovered, for about 60 minutes, or until the vegetables are done and tender. Check for seasoning and serve hot.

WILD BOAR

Wild boar, along with feral (wild) hogs, are found in about twenty-three states and are estimated to number over 2 million. Like domestic swine, these critters are not native to North America. Originally domesticated and then released into the wild, these animals are now hybrids. I absolutely love the taste of a great wild boar soup. I like it even more cooked on the grill!

Sambuca Hills Deer Burger & Mac Soup

1 pound deer burger
1 chopped yellow onion
2 minced garlic cloves
$^1/_2$ green bell pepper, chopped
1 teaspoon oil
2 cups canned diced tomatoes with juice
6 cups beef stock
$^1/_2$ cup tomato sauce
1 teaspoon Worcestershire sauce
1 teaspoon dried basil
1 teaspoon salt
Pepper to taste
1 cup uncooked elbow macaroni
1 cup canned red kidney beans, drained and rinsed

In a large soup pot over medium heat, combine the meat, onions, garlic, and bell pepper. Cook, breaking the meat up with a wooden spoon, until the meat is browned and the vegetables are tender (about 10 minutes). Add the oil if needed to prevent the mixture from sticking. Add the remaining ingredients and bring to a boil. Lower the heat and simmer, uncovered, stirring occasionally, for about 30 minutes or until the macaroni is tender and the flavors are blended.

Jake & Derby Haze's Cabin Moose Meat Stew

1 pound moose round steak, trimmed and cubed
1 tablespoon vegetable oil
$1/4$ cup butter
$1/4$ cup flour
2 cups beef consommé
$1/2$ cup chopped carrots
$1/2$ cup chopped onions
$1/2$ cup chopped celery
1 cup chopped red potatoes
1 teaspoon Kitchen Bouquet browning sauce
$1/2$ teaspoon black pepper
5 ounces fresh tomatoes, seeded and chopped
1 16-ounce package frozen soup mixed vegetables, with potatoes

Brown the moose meat on all sides in the oil in a large skillet; drain. Melt the butter in a saucepan. Stir in the flour. Cook until smooth and bubbly, stirring constantly. Stir in the consommé gradually. Cook until thickened, stirring constantly. Add the carrots, onions, celery, potatoes, Kitchen Bouquet, and pepper to the broth mixture and mix well. Bring to a boil; reduce the heat and simmer for about 5 minutes, stirring occasionally. Add the moose meat, tomatoes, and frozen vegetables, and mix gently. Simmer, covered, for about 15 minutes, stirring occasionally. Taste and adjust for seasoning. Serve hot.

Cousin Rick's Two Days at Camp Elk Soup

This is a two-day hunters' stew—very good!

2 pounds elk stew meat
1 large marrow bone
1 tablespoon plus 1 teaspoon salt
2 cups canned tomatoes with juice
1 onion, peeled and quartered
1 stalk celery, chopped
3 parsley sprigs
6 whole peppercorns
1 bay leaf
2 cups shredded pared beets
3 cups coarsely shredded cabbage
1½ cups thickly sliced carrots
1 cup chopped onions
2 teaspoons dill weed
¼ cup cider vinegar
2 tablespoons sugar
Sour cream

First Day

Place the elk meat, marrow bone, 1 tablespoon salt, and 2 quarts water in a deep kettle. Cover, bring to a boil, and skim the surface. Reduce the heat; simmer, covered, for about 60 minutes. Add the tomatoes, quartered onions, celery, parsley, peppercorns, and bay leaf; simmer, covered, for about 2 hours. Remove from heat. Lift out the meat and set aside. Remove the marrow bone and discard. Strain the soup; skim the fat. Return the soup and meat to the kettle. Add the beets, cabbage, carrots, chopped onion, dill, vinegar, sugar, and 1 teaspoon salt; bring to a boil. Reduce the heat and simmer for about 60 minutes. Remove from the heat and refrigerate overnight.

Second Day

Remove the meat from the soup and cut it into cubes. Return it to the soup and heat the soup to a boil. Let the soup simmer for about 30 minutes before serving. Top each bowl of soup with a spoonful of sour cream.

Nibbles Wild Pig Stew

1 large Spanish onion, coarsely chopped
4 garlic cloves, medium chopped
3 tablespoons extra virgin olive oil
2 tablespoons sea salt
2 pounds wild pig roast, cut into cubes
1 tablespoon black pepper
2 tablespoons Frank's Red Hot Sauce
2 tablespoons Worcestershire sauce
4 cups stewed tomatoes with basil and garlic
1 pound fresh mushrooms, sliced
12 large potatoes, peeled and cubed
1 pound baby carrots, chunked
3 stalks celery, chunked
1 large green bell pepper, seeded and chunked
1 large orange bell pepper, seeded and chunked
1 tablespoon white pepper
3 tablespoons paprika
$1/4$ cup oregano flakes
6 cups water

Sauté the onions and garlic in olive oil with a generous dash of sea salt until golden; remove from pan. In the same pan, sear the wild boar cubes with a small dash of sea salt and a pinch of pepper and a generous dash of Frank's Red Hot Sauce and Worcestershire sauce.

In a large soup pot, combine all ingredients and fill with water to about 2 inches from the rim. Cover with lid. Bring to boil over medium heat. Reduce the heat to low and simmer until the carrots and potatoes are tender, stirring often, about 3 hours. Check for seasoning and serve hot.

Tooter's Tavern Venison & Black-Eyed Pea Soup

2 pounds deer burger
$^1/_2$ cup green bell peppers, chopped
$^1/_2$ cup butter
$^1/_2$ cup all-purpose flour
2 quarts water
2 cups chopped tomatoes
16 ounces frozen black-eyed peas
1 cup chopped yellow onion
1 cup diced carrots
1 cup diced celery
2 tablespoons beef bouillon granules
1 tablespoon fresh ground pepper
$^1/_2$ teaspoon seasoning salt
$^1/_2$ teaspoon garlic powder
2 cups cooked white rice

Brown the deer burger and green pepper in a large skillet; drain and set aside. Melt the butter in a Dutch oven; add flour, whisking until smooth. Cook and stir constantly for about a minute. Gradually add in the water and stir until all is bubbly. Stir in the deer burger mixture and all the remaining ingredients except the cooked rice. Bring the soup to a boil; cover and lower heat to a simmer for about 60 minutes. Add the rice during the last 15 minutes of cooking.

Winchester 30-30 Buffalo Steak Soup

2 pounds buffalo sirloin steaks

I pound lean ground buffalo

I cup chopped celery

I cup chopped onions

I cup chopped fresh tomatoes

I teaspoon celery salt

$^1/_2$ teaspoon spicy seasoning salt

I teaspoon red cayenne pepper (add more if you're like me)

$^1/_2$ teaspoon black pepper

$^1/_2$ teaspoon Kitchen Bouquet browning sauce

4 tablespoons oil

6 tablespoons flour

6 cups beef stock

Cut the steak into cubes and brown in a large skillet. Add the ground buffalo and cook until no longer pink. Sauté the vegetables and seasonings; then add to brown meat. In a separate pan, heat the oil, add the flour, and stir until very brown (but not burned). Pour half of the stock into the flour and stir until smooth. Pour the remaining stock over the meat; bring to a gentle boil. Combine all ingredients, cover, and reduce the heat to a simmer. Simmer for about 2 hours, check for seasoning, and serve hot.

Billy's Been in the Beer Caribou Pizza Soup

1 pound ground caribou
2 26-ounce cans condensed tomato soup, undiluted
6^1/$_2$ cups water
28 ounces meaty spaghetti sauce
1 tablespoon Italian seasoning
2 cups shredded cheddar cheese

In a Dutch oven, cook the ground caribou over medium heat until it is no longer pink; drain. Add the soup, water, spaghetti sauce, and seasoning; bring to a boil. Reduce the heat and simmer, uncovered, for about 20 minutes. Add the cheese and simmer until melted. Garnish the soup with additional cheese. This soup is great with garlic bread and is a favorite served every year at my winter cabin.

Cousin Rick's Wild Game Jerky & Rice Soup

10 sticks of dried smoked wild game jerky
1 quart boiling water
1 tablespoon lard or vegetable oil
^{3}/$_4$ cup rice
1 yellow onion, chopped
^{1}/$_2$ teaspoon salt
3 ripe tomatoes, chopped
1 whole dried chile
1 sweet pepper, cored, seeded, and diced

In a stockpot, add boiling water and wild game jerky. Let sit for about 15 minutes. Remove from the water and cut into small pieces. Return to pot and simmer on low heat. In a large skillet, add the lard, rice, and onions, and lightly sprinkle with salt (remember, jerky has salt). Brown the rice and cook the onions until slightly browned.

Add the tomatoes and chile pepper. Simmer for about 10 minutes. Add the sweet pepper to the stockpot. Simmer the soup for about 20 minutes or until the rice is tender and cooked. Remove the whole chile pepper before serving.

Gusto Bear Stew

1 pound bear roast, cut into 1-inch chunks
2 tablespoons flour
1 tablespoon corn oil
1 white onion, finely chopped
2 garlic cloves, minced
2 carrots, thinly sliced
1 pound potatoes, diced
3 cups diced tomatoes, with their juices
3 tablespoons molasses
3 tablespoons red wine vinegar
1 teaspoon ginger
Seasoned salt and pepper to taste

Dredge the bear meat in flour and cook over medium heat. Cook the meat for about 5 minutes or until lightly browned. Remove to a plate and set aside. Reduce the heat to moderate, add the onion and garlic to the pan, and sauté for about 5 minutes. Add the carrots and cook for about 3 minutes more. Add the potatoes, tomatoes, molasses, vinegar, ginger, salt, and pepper. Bring to a boil and reduce the heat to a simmer. Cover and simmer for about 30 minutes, or until the potatoes are tender. Return the bear meat to the pan, cover, and simmer for about 15 minutes more. Serve hot after checking for seasoning.

Durango Daff's Stew

$^1/_3$ cup flour

1 teaspoon salt

$^1/_2$ teaspoon pepper

3 pounds lean wild sheep stew meat, cubed

3 tablespoons vegetable oil

1 10.5-ounce can condensed beef consommé, undiluted

2 onions, halved and sliced

1 cup red wine

1 garlic clove, minced

$^1/_2$ teaspoon dill weed

2 6.5-ounce jars marinated artichoke hearts, drained and chopped

20 fresh mushrooms, halved

4 cups cooked noodles

In a shallow bowl, combine flour, salt, and pepper. Add sheep meat and toss to coat. In a skillet, brown the wild sheep meat in oil. Transfer to a slow cooker with a slotted spoon. Gradually add the consommé to the skillet. Bring to a boil and stir to loosen brown bits from the pan. Stir in the onions, wine, garlic, and dill. Pour over meat. Cover and simmer on low for about 8 hours, or until the meat is nearly tender. Stir in the artichokes and mushrooms; cook about 30 minutes longer, or until heated through. Check for seasoning and serve over hot noodles.

Jezebel Jenny's Long Branch Buffalo Cider Stew

2 pounds buffalo stew meat, cubed

3 tablespoons flour

2 teaspoons salt

$^1/_4$ teaspoon pepper

$^1/_2$ teaspoon dried thyme

3 tablespoons bacon fat

3 potatoes, peeled and quartered

4 carrots, quartered

2 large yellow onions, sliced

1 stalk celery, sliced

1 apple, chopped

2 cups apple cider

1 tablespoon vinegar

$^1/_2$ cup cold beer

Coat the buffalo meat cubes with a mixture of flour, salt, pepper, and thyme. In a large skillet, brown the meat in bacon fat. Drain off the fat. Place the vegetables and chopped apple in a large slow cooker. Place the meat on top of the vegetables. Combine the apple cider and vinegar, and pour it over the meat. Cover and cook for about 12 hours on low heat. Turn the cooker to high heat. Blend $^1/_2$ cup of cold beer with $^1/_4$ cup flour. Stir this mixture into the stew. Cook for another 20 minutes, or until the stew is thickened. Check for seasoning and serve hot to a bunch of hungry outlaws.

MOOSE

Moose is the largest member of the venison family. These big boys stand about $6^1/_2$ feet at the shoulder. The moose is a native of North America, and the meat tastes similar to elk. Moose meat is great for roasting and of course is one of my favorite meats for soups and stews. Plus the racks are cool!

Northern Exposure Moose Stew

I cup sun-dried tomatoes
2 pounds moose stew meat
1 1/2 pounds potatoes, cut in halves
I large white onion, cut in wedges
About 25 baby carrots
2 cups beer
2 teaspoons Holland Grill seasoning salt
I bay leaf
1/4 cup water
2 tablespoons flour

Rehydrate the tomatoes as directed on the package, drain, and coarsely chop. Mix the tomatoes and remaining ingredients in a large soup pan, except for the water and flour. Cover and simmer on low heat for about 8 hours, or until the meat and vegetables are tender. Mix the water and flour together and slowly add to the stew. Cover and simmer for another 20 minutes, or until the stew slightly thickens. Remove the bay leaf and serve hot after checking again for seasoning.

Camp Apache Buffalo Balls
& Cabbage Soup

2 pounds ground buffalo
2 tablespoons minced onions
1/4 teaspoon mustard
1/4 teaspoon soy sauce
1/4 teaspoon seasoned salt
1/4 teaspoon white pepper
I tablespoon dry red wine
2 cups beef stock
2 large cabbage leaves, diced
I tomato, diced
1/2 teaspoon fresh parsley

Combine the ground buffalo meat, onions, mustard, soy sauce, salt, and pepper; mix thoroughly. Form the meat into small meatballs. Add wine to the stock and bring to a boil. Add the meatballs to the stock, one at a time. Bring the mixture back to a boil. Cook the meatballs for about 5 minutes; remove them to a soup bowl. Add the cabbage and the tomatoes to the stock. Simmer for about 5 minutes. Check the stock for seasoning, pour over the buffalo balls, and garnish with parsley.

Punta Cana Wild Goat Hunter's Paradise Soup

I brought this great recipe back from the Dominican Republic.
I have changed a few of the ingredients to make it more user-friendly
for my hillbilly buddies.

1 pound wild goat meat, diced
Bacon fat
1 cup diced onions
1 cup diced carrots
1 cup chopped celery
$^1/_2$ cup cooked peas
6 shrimp, peeled and deveined
3 potatoes, peeled and cubed
2 garlic cloves, minced
3 cups diced tomatoes with juices
2 cups tomato juice
1 teaspoon chili powder
1 tablespoon sugar
1 tablespoon coconut milk
1 teaspoon sea salt
1 teaspoon pepper
1 teaspoon cayenne

In a large soup pot, brown the meat in bacon fat. Add the remaining ingredients and simmer on low for about 8 hours, stirring often.

(I had my first sample of this soup made by Chef Wendiual at a beach party in the spring of 2006. Although he would not tell me all of his spices, this soup is pretty close. Feel free to have fun with this one and make it as thick or thin as you wish.)

Chef Jerry Riggs's Elk-in-Rut Soup

1 cup chopped onion
1 cup chopped celery
$^1/_4$ cup butter
2 cups beef broth
2 cups chicken broth
1 teaspoon baking soda
$^1/_4$ cup cornstarch
$^1/_4$ cup water
1$^1/_2$ cups sauerkraut, rinsed and drained
4 cups milk
4 cups dried elk meat, chopped
2 cups shredded Swiss cheese
Salt and pepper to taste
Rye croutons for garnish

Sauté the onions and celery in butter until tender. Transfer to a large crock. Stir in the beef and chicken broths and add the baking soda. Combine the cornstarch and water and add to the crock. Stir in the sauerkraut, milk, and dried elk pieces. Cover the crock and cook on high for about 4 hours. Stir in the cheese and simmer for another 30 minutes. Season the soup with salt and pepper and serve in bowls garnished with rye croutons.

Alamo Deer Soup

1 pound lean boneless deer stew meat, trimmed of fat and cut into
$^1/_2$-inch cubes
4 cups beef broth
2 cups water
1 16-ounce package frozen fajita-style vegetables, thawed
1 14$^1/_2$-ounce can Mexican-style thick and chunky tomato sauce
1 15-ounce can pinto beans, rinsed and drained
2 teaspoon cumin
1 15-ounce can black beans, rinsed and drained
$^1/_4$ teaspoon seasoned salt
$^1/_4$ teaspoon garlic pepper
Sour cream
Chopped avocado
Shredded Monterey Jack cheese

In a large slow cooker, combine the venison, broth, water, vegetables, tomato sauce, pinto beans, and cumin. Cover and cook on low for about 8 hours, or until the venison is tender. Stir in the black beans, seasoned salt, and garlic powder. Heat, covered, for about 15 minutes. Serve this great soup with sour cream, avocado, and cheese.

UNCLE MARVIN

One day Cousin Rick was walking down Main Street when he saw Uncle Marvin driving a brand-new pickup truck. Marvin pulled up to him with a coon-eating grin. "Uncle Marvin, where'd you get that truck?"

"Erma Sue gave it to me," Marvin replied.

"She gave it to you! I knew she was kinda sweet on ya, but a new truck?"

"Well, Rick, let me tell you what happened. We were driving out on County Road 16, in the middle of nowhere. Erma Sue pulled off the road, put the truck in four-wheel drive, and headed into the deep timber. She parked the truck, got out, threw off all her clothes and said, 'Marvin, take whatever you want.' So I took the truck!"

"Uncle Marvin, you're a smart man! Them clothes woulda never fit you," replied Cousin Rick.

Dusty Kramer's Caribou and Mashed Taters Wild Game Stew

3 tablespoons bacon drippings

2 pounds caribou stew meat, chopped

12 small white onions, peeled

12 baby carrots

5 tablespoons flour

2 teaspoons salt

$^1/_2$ teaspoon pepper

1 tablespoon prepared mustard

1 small bay leaf

2 cups beef stock

1 cup vegetable juice

2 cups seasoned mashed potatoes, with skins on

Heat the bacon drippings in a heavy skillet over medium-low heat; add the caribou meat and brown, turning frequently. Remove the meat to a large casserole dish. Add the onions and carrots to the meat in the casserole dish. Combine the flour, salt, pepper, mustard, bay leaf, stock, and vegetable juice in a skillet over medium-low heat; simmer for about 25 minutes. Remove the bay leaf and pour the sauce over the vegetables. Cover the casserole and bake at 325 degrees for about $2^1/_2$ hours. Remove the casserole from the oven and arrange the mashed potatoes around the edges. Increase the oven temperature to 400 degrees and bake for about 20 minutes longer, or until the mashed taters are good and brown. Serve hot from the oven.

J.B.'s Barbecue Antelope
Slow-Cooked Stew

2 pounds antelope stew meat

3 tablespoons bacon fat

I cup sliced onion

$^1/_2$ cup chopped green bell pepper

I large garlic clove, minced

$^1/_2$ teaspoon salt

$^1/_2$ teaspoon pepper

2 cups beef stock

2 cups crushed tomatoes with juices

$^1/_2$ cup fresh mushrooms, sliced

$^1/_3$ cup **BBQ** sauce

3 tablespoons cornstarch

$^1/_4$ cup beer

If the meat is in large pieces, cut into smaller cubes. Heat the bacon fat in a skillet over medium heat. Sauté the onion, pepper, and garlic in the hot fat. Add salt, pepper, beef stock, tomatoes, mushrooms, and BBQ sauce. Cover and cook on low for about 10 hours, stirring about every hour or so. Mix the cornstarch with the beer and stir into the stew about 20 minutes before it is finished cooking. Serve this great stew over cooked wild rice.

The Last Frontier Ranch Antelope Stew with Beer

3 pounds antelope stew meat, cut in small cubes

8 cups thinly sliced onions

3 garlic cloves, crushed and minced

1/2 cup butter

1/4 cup flour

6 ounces tomato paste

8 ounces mushrooms, quartered

1 tablespoon brown sugar

2 teaspoons salt

1 1/2 teaspoons dried thyme leaves

1 teaspoon ground black pepper

1 bay leaf

3 cups beer

In a large Dutch oven over medium heat, brown antelope cubes on all sides. Remove the meat cubes as they brown. Combine the onions, garlic, and 1/4 cup butter in the same pan; reduce heat to low and cook until the onions are golden brown, stirring occasionally. Combine the remaining butter and flour in a heavy skillet. Cook over low heat, stirring occasionally, until the mixture turns a rich brown. Return the meat cubes to the Dutch oven with onions. Add the tomato paste, mushrooms, brown sugar, salt, thyme, pepper, and bay leaf. Slowly pour the beer into the browned flour mixture, stirring often. Combine the flour and beer mixture with the meat and onion mixture and mix well. Heat the stew to boiling. Cover the Dutch oven with foil and then cover with the lid. Cook for about 2 hours, remove the bay leaf, and serve hot.

Horseshoe Canyon Deer Burger Stew

2 pounds deer burger, browned, drained
I chopped red onion
3 chopped green onions
6 carrots, peeled and sliced
6 medium potatoes, peeled and diced
I teaspoon minced garlic
Seasoned salt and black pepper to taste
I tablespoon Gravy Master
I tablespoon instant beef bouillon

Place all the ingredients in a pot. Add water to cover. Cover and simmer lightly for about 60 minutes, or until the vegetables are tender. Check the stew for seasoning and serve hot.

Wild Goat and Sheep

Wild goat meat is great to cook with and eat if the hunter is very careful to give the meat the proper care. Bighorn sheep is an excellent wild game meat, too. Like all game, these animals should be cleaned and cooled promptly. Take care when dragging out big game such as a large bighorn; study and make sure you or your guide knows that dirt is not good for game meat. Many hunters have wasted good meat because it was dragged behind a quad-runner stuffing it with dirt, leaves, and muddy snow.

Coffee Creek Bear and Beer Oven Stew

2 tablespoons bacon drippings

1 cup sliced yellow onion

2 pounds lean bear roast, cut in 1-inch cubes

1 tablespoon flour

1 cup beer

2 tablespoons vinegar

1 teaspoon garlic salt

$^1/_2$ teaspoon ground black pepper

$^1/_2$ teaspoon sugar

1 bay leaf

$^1/_4$ teaspoon thyme, crumbled

Preheat the oven to 350 degrees. In a Dutch oven over medium-high heat, melt the bacon fat; brown the onions. Remove the onions from the pan; add the bear meat and brown on all sides. Sprinkle the bear meat with flour; add the onions and remaining ingredients and stir well. Cover tightly and bake for about $2^1/_2$ hours, or until very tender.

Old Glenderey's Slow Cooker Herbed Boar Stew

3 pounds wild pig stew roast

$^1/_4$ cup flour

Salt and pepper

6 slices bacon, diced

2 onions, chopped

2 cups beef stock

$^1/_4$ teaspoon ground cloves

$^1/_4$ teaspoon ground nutmeg

2 tablespoons wine vinegar

2 tablespoons brown sugar

1 teaspoon dried oregano

1 teaspoon dried thyme

6 ounces small whole mushrooms

Cut the wild pig meat into cubes, and dredge in flour mixed with a little salt and pepper. Place the bacon in a skillet and fry a few minutes. Add the pig meat and brown on all sides. Add the onions and cook for about 3 more minutes. Transfer all to a large slow cooker. Stir in the remaining ingredients and add water if needed. Cover and cook on low heat for about 10 hours. You may thicken the juices with a mixture of flour and cold water if desired. This wild boar stew is great with potatoes or noodles.

Black Rush Diamond Tangy Caribou Stew

2 pounds caribou steaks, cut in 1-inch cubes
1 cup sliced carrots
1 medium onion, sliced
1 8-ounce can tomato sauce
1/2 cup sliced mushrooms
1/4 cup bacon bits (real)
1/4 cup brown sugar
1/4 cup vinegar
1 tablespoon Worcestershire sauce
1/2 cup beef stock
1/2 cup beer
1 1-ounce shot Jack Daniels Kentucky bourbon
1 teaspoon seasoned salt
1 tablespoon cornstarch
2 tablespoons cold water
Fried potatoes with onions

Place the first thirteen ingredients into a large slow cooker, stir, cover, and cook on low until the meat is tender, about 9 hours. Turn the cooker to high. Combine the cornstarch and cold water; add to the soup mixture. Cook and stir until thickened and bubbly. Serve over hot fried potatoes with onions.

Wild Bill Gordon's Fat Man's Buffalo Stew

I pound buffalo round steak, cut in 1-inch slices
I 10½-ounce can tomato soup
I tablespoon tomato paste
½ cup beer
I tablespoon Kitchen Bouquet browning sauce
3 medium potatoes, diced
3 medium carrots, peeled and diced
¼ cup chopped onion
½ teaspoon seasoned salt
½ teaspoon black pepper
I cup frozen peas
I cup frozen corn

Combine the buffalo meat, tomato soup, tomato paste, beer, Kitchen Bouquet, potatoes, carrots, onions, seasoned salt, and pepper in a slow cooker. Cover and cook on low for about 10 hours. Add the peas and corn in the last 30 minutes of cooking. Serve stew over buttermilk biscuits.

DUTCH-OVEN TIPS FROM COUSIN RICK AND HIS FRIENDS AT CAMP CHEF

Whenever I get the opportunity to use my Camp Chef Lewis & Clark Dutch oven, be it for the backyard summer cookout, on a camping trip, or on a hunting trip, there are some easy-to-learn skills that make the experience a real success. My preferred choice of Dutch ovens are made by Camp Chef out of Logan, Utah. These boys will tell you that an unseasoned Dutch oven is gray in color, where a seasoned oven (like theirs) will be shiny, smooth, and black in appearance, both inside and out. And don't forget about the lid! The ideal Dutch oven has three legs for standing and a tight-fitting lid with a lip of an inch or so sticking up on the outer rim. This lip on the lid lets the cook place the hot coals or briquettes on top of the oven, thus creating an oven with the heat coming from the bottom as well as the top and radiating to the sides. Dutch ovens have a handle on top of the lid that makes checking your soups and stews easy. I would recommend having a clean board or a couple of pieces of wood available to set the lid on after you carefully remove it. I use a folded piece of paper towel to wipe around the seam where the lid and oven meet. This reduces the possibility of me getting any ash in my stew. You can lift out the whole oven by the wire bail, away from the fire while you check your food. I use pliers to push the fire material away from the handle; then I lift the lid straight up and off. Even though the lid is covered with hot coals, a wire hook may be used to lift it. Work quickly to replace the lid before too much heat is lost. Adjust the coals if they are too hot by moving part of them away from the top or bottom of the oven. If your soup is not cooking fast enough, add more hot coals. Put the oven back into the cooking position and cook until your soup or stew is ready to serve. If any sticky remains are left in the oven, clean as well as possible with cooking oil and paper towels. Then add warm soapy water and wash with a dishcloth or a large thick sponge with an abrasive backing. After all the food particles are good and loose, I rinse the oven thoroughly and dry it completely with a paper towel. Don't forget to go over the outside of the oven and lid with paper towels, removing all dirt and any moisture. I cover my oven thoroughly with cooking oil, starting with the inside first. I remove any excess oil and store it with the lid in position on the upright oven. This way my oven will be ready for the next use. If the oil inside the oven gets rancid, remove it with warm soapy water and follow the cleaning instructions above.

Almost all outdoor areas have firewood available. Most wood is good for cooking if it holds up in a bank of hot coals for some time. If the fire material burns too quickly and turns to ash almost immediately, it will not work for your Dutch oven cooking. You have to prepare a fire large enough to burn down into coals—enough to cover the top of the oven as well as underneath. Half-burned and burning material smokes, is difficult to handle and control, and does not have the sustained heat needed for cooking. I use a long-handled shovel for moving the coals. When a hot bank of coals is ready, spread a layer of coals over your oven. The layers of coals can get too hot; only experience will help you to decide when the temperature of the coals is right. Of the many ways to cook wild game soups and stews, I truly love using my Dutch oven. A Dutch oven cooks and bakes deliciously using a method that cannot be duplicated. I find it is the most dependable way to prepare a complete meal for a few or many hunters in an outdoor situation. A soup or stew prepared in my Dutch oven is easily served from the oven itself and can be cleaned with minimum effort. So what are you waiting on? Get out there and get yourself a Dutch oven! Start at www. campchef.com!

So far I have written many tips and instructions on cooking your wild game soups and stews. Here's one for you to use the next time you have a crowd around and you're waiting for some vittles. According to a news report, a certain school in Iowa was recently faced with a unique problem. It seems a number of teenage lads thought that it was cool to go to the boys room, put on Chap Stick and then press their lips to the mirror leaving dozens of little lip prints. Every night, the maintenance man would remove them, and the next day the lads would put them back. Finally the principal decided that something had to be done. He called all the boys to the washroom and met them there with the maintenance man. He explained that all these lip prints were causing a major problem for the custodian who had to clean the mirrors every night. To demonstrate how difficult it was to clean the mirrors, he asked the maintenance man to show the boys how much effort was required. He took out a long-handled squeegee, dipped it in the toilet, and cleaned the mirror with it! Since then, there have been no lip prints on the mirror. The moral of this story: There are teachers, and then there are educators!

Fremont Village Wild Goat Stew

3 pounds potatoes, peeled and cut into $^1/_2$-inch slices
2 pounds boneless wild goat shoulder, cut into 2-inch cubes
2 onions, sliced
Salt and pepper to taste
I cup beer
I cup red wine
I cup beef stock
I cup chopped fresh parsley

Set half the potatoes aside in a pot of water. Combine the remaining potatoes, wild goat meat, onions, salt, pepper, beer, wine, and stock in a large pot. Cover and bring to a boil over high heat. Reduce the heat and simmer, covered, for about 60 minutes. Add the reserved potatoes and add additional liquid if the stew is too dry. Simmer, covered, until the second batch of potatoes is tender. Check the stew for seasoning, garnish with parsley, and serve hot.

Thunder Basin Wild Goat Delicious Stew

- 2 pounds wild goat meat, cut up
- 2 tablespoons oil
- I teaspoon sugar
- 3 tablespoons flour
- I cup red wine
- I large onion, chopped
- I cup beef consommé
- 2 cups beef stock
- I6 ounces chopped tomatoes
- I tablespoon fresh thyme
- I teaspoon fresh rosemary
- I bay leaf
- 3 carrots, chopped
- 3 celery stalks, chopped
- 3 potatoes, cut in cubes

Cut up and dry the wild goat meat. Heat the oil in a Dutch oven and brown the meat for 3 to 5 minutes. Turn the meat, add sugar, and continue cooking for about 3 minutes, or until brown. Add the flour to the meat and cook for about 2 minutes. Remove the meat from the pot and deglaze the pot with red wine. Reduce the wine to about $1/4$ cup. Add the onions and sauté for about 2 minutes. Then add the consommé, stock, tomatoes, thyme, rosemary, and bay leaf. Cover, reduce the heat, and simmer on low for about $1^1/2$ hours. Add the vegetables and bring to a boil. Reduce the heat and simmer on low for another 60 minutes. Check the stew for seasoning before serving.

Tongass Toby's Moose Heart Stew

1 large moose heart
Bacon drippings
1 stalk celery
1 cup mushrooms
2 large onions
1 large green bell pepper
2 cups whole tomatoes, chopped with juice
4 cups tomato sauce
Garlic salt and pepper to taste

Trim off all sinew and fat from the heart. Parboil for about 2 hours, or until the heart meat is good and tender. Chop the heart into stew-sized cubes. Brown the meat in bacon drippings in a large skillet. Dice the celery, mushrooms, onions, and pepper. Fry with the meat and bacon drippings until tender. Add the tomatoes and sauce to the mixture. Simmer on low heat until all is tender. If the stew is too thick, add beer. Add garlic salt and pepper to taste and serve hot.

Camp Charles Venison Stew

3 pounds venison, chopped
$1/4$ cup fat
Salt
$1/2$ tablespoon ground black pepper
Flour
3 slices salt pork
$1/4$ cup hot beer
$1/2$ tablespoon vinegar
$1/2$ cup celery, chopped
$1/4$ cup carrots, chopped
1 apple, chopped
$1/2$ tablespoon lemon juice
1 tablespoon Accent

Cover all sides of the venison meat in fat, salt, pepper, and flour. Brown the seasoned venison and the salt pork in hot fat in a large Dutch oven until all sides of the meat are browned. Add the beer and vinegar to the meat mixture, cover, and simmer on low heat for about 3 hours, adding more beer if needed. Add the remaining ingredients and simmer on low, covered, for about 45 minutes, or until all is tender. Check for seasoning and serve hot. This is a great camp stew that is even better reheated the next day.

Cody's Creek Buffalo Italian Sausage Stew

1 pound hot buffalo Italian sausage, chopped
1 package frozen mixed vegetables
2 cups canned Italian-style tomatoes, diced
2 zucchini, sliced
2 cups canned mushrooms, drained and sliced
4 garlic cloves, minced
2 tablespoons Italian-style tomato paste
Garlic salt and pepper to taste

Heat a large skillet over high heat until hot. Add the buffalo sausage and cook until all sides are brown. Pour off any drippings. Combine the cooked sausage, frozen veggies, tomatoes, zucchini, mushrooms, and garlic cloves in a large slow cooker. Cover and cook on low heat for about 5 hours or until the zucchini is tender. Stir in the tomato paste. Cover and cook for another 45 minutes, or until the juices of the stew have thickened. Season with garlic salt and pepper and serve hot.

DEER MATING
One afternoon last fall, Cousin Rick took his wife, Becky, to a white-tail antler show. As they strolled through the show enjoying the sights, they noticed a seminar on the life cycle of deer. They thought this sounded interesting so they went in and joined the seminar already in progress. About that time the speaker stated that a dominant buck might mate a hundred or more times in a single season. Becky's mouth dropped open and she said, "Wow! A hundred times in a season, that's more than once a day! You could really learn from these deer." Cousin Rick turned to Becky and said, "Raise your hand and inquire if it was a hundred times with the same doe."

Axe Handle Caribou Soup

4 cups beef stock
I cup tomato paste
I teaspoon salt
I teaspoon ground black pepper
$1/2$ teaspoon ground cayenne pepper
I green bell pepper, chopped
I red bell pepper, chopped
2 cups fresh corn kernels
I tablespoon vegetable oil
I onion, diced
4 garlic cloves, minced
I pound ground caribou

In a large soup pot over high heat, combine the stock, tomato paste, salt, ground black pepper, cayenne pepper, green bell pepper, red bell pepper, and corn. Bring to a boil, reduce the heat, and simmer at a slow boil for about 40 minutes. In a large saucepan over medium heat, combine the oil, onion, and garlic, sauté for about 5 minutes, and then add to the simmering soup. In the same saucepan over medium heat, sauté the ground caribou meat until well browned, and add to the soup. Stir the soup well for about 20 more minutes, check for seasoning, and serve hot.

"This Ain't Hollywood!" Wild Boar Jambalaya

I pound ground wild pig
I pound smoked sausage, chopped
I onion, chopped
3 stalks celery, chopped
I garlic clove, chopped
I medium head cabbage, chopped
I cup stewed tomatoes, chopped
2 cups chicken broth
I cup uncooked rice
Garlic salt and pepper to taste

In a large stockpot over medium high heat, combine the ground wild pig, smoked sausage, onion, celery, and garlic. Cook until the pig is evenly browned. Stir in the cabbage, tomatoes, chicken broth, and rice. Season with garlic salt and pepper to taste. Bring the jambalaya to a boil, and then reduce the heat to low. Cover and simmer for about 45 minutes, or until the rice is done.

Savage Land Outdoors Big Horn Soup

4 cups chicken broth
4 cups beef broth
3 pounds wild sheep shanks
I carrot, chopped
I onion, chopped
I celery stalk, chopped
I bay leaf
3 tablespoons olive oil
I onion, sliced
$^3/_4$ cups rice-shaped pasta
I pound fresh spinach, chopped
Salt and pepper to taste
Parmesan cheese, freshly grated

Bring the broths to a boil in a heavy, large saucepan over high heat. Add the wild sheep shanks, carrots, chopped onions, celery, and bay leaf. Bring this mixture to a boil. Reduce the heat and simmer on low until the shank meat is tender. Transfer the meat to a plate and cool slightly. Remove the meat from the bone and chop into small pieces. Strain the cooking liquid and reserve. In the same pot, heat olive oil over medium heat. Add the sliced onion and sauté for about 5 minutes. Add the reserved cooking liquid, meat, and pasta. Cook the soup over medium heat until the pasta is tender but still firm to the bite. Add the spinach and cook until wilted. Season the soup to taste with salt and pepper. Top the soup with the grated Parmesan cheese before serving.

Ruttin' Critter in the Beans Soup

*I had the privilege of eating this wild pig soup while hunting a reserve
in southeastern Illinois. Very good!*

9 pounds dry white beans
3 pounds wild pig hocks
Beer
1 1/2 pounds chopped carrots
2 pounds diced onions
1/4 cup sugar
4 crushed garlic cloves
1 pound soup gravy base, beef
1 teaspoon ground black pepper
4 bay leaves

Pick over the beans, removing any foreign matter. Wash the
beans thoroughly in cold water. Cover the beans with water and bring
to a boil. Place the boar hocks in enough beer to cover. Simmer for
about 60 minutes. Remove the hocks from the beer and allow to cool.
Remove the lean meat and chop into small soup-sized pieces. Add
the remaining ingredients, including the cooked beans, to the hock
liquid and simmer for about 4 hours. Check the soup for seasoning
and remove the bay leaves. Serve the soup hot with fresh cornbread.

Apogee Valley Antelope Soup

3 pound antelope rump roast
2 large white onions
4 quarts water
Salt and pepper taste
1 horseradish root
1 loaf crusty French bread

Brown the antelope roast in a large heavy stockpot. Brown
chopped onions after the roast. Cover the roast and onions with the
water. Boil until the antelope roast is tender. Remove the roast from
heat and allow to cool. Shred the cooled roast into small strips and
pieces. Return the shredded meat to the stock and season the soup

to taste. Slice the bread on diagonal and float on stock. Take the cleaned fresh horseradish and grate it into the soup. Make sure to taste occasionally until you have the flavor you desire. Serve this great soup hot.

Chubby Davis's Wild Game Feed Soup

The soup that made Alexandra, Missouri, famous!

1 pound deer burger
1 cup diced onions
1 cup chopped celery
1 cup chopped baby carrots
2 cloves garlic, minced
1 28-ounce can tomatoes, chopped and undrained
1 15-ounce can red kidney beans, undrained
2 cups water
Beef bouillon cubes or concentrate, undiluted, that would dilute to
    make 5 cups of stock
1/4 cup parsley, minced
1 teaspoon Accent
1/2 teaspoon oregano, crushed
1/4 teaspoon ground black pepper
2 cups cabbage, shredded
1 cup green beans, chopped
1/2 cup small elbow macaroni
1/2 teaspoon basil, crushed
Parmesan cheese as a garnish

Brown the deer burger in a large heavy kettle, draining off any fat. Add all the remaining ingredients except the cabbage, green beans, macaroni, basil, and Parmesan cheese. Bring to a boil; then reduce the heat and simmer for about 30 minutes. Add the cabbage, green beans, and macaroni. Bring to a boil again; then reduce the heat and simmer until the vegetables are tender. When ready to serve, stir in the basil and top the soup with the Parmesan cheese.

After eating an entire bull elk, a mountain lion felt so good he started roaring. He roared and he roared, until an elk hunter came along and shot him. The moral of this story: When you're full of bull, keep your mouth shut!

Rambo's Revenge Razorback Soup

1 pound ground wild pig meat
1 cup chopped white onions
1 tablespoon olive oil
3 cloves garlic, diced
2 cups beef broth
1 28-ounce can tomatoes, with the tomatoes squeezed and chopped
    into small pieces and the juice reserved
1 apple, unpeeled, cored, and chopped
2 canned whole jalapeños, sliced thin
10 pimiento-stuffed olives, halved
$1/4$ cup yellow raisins
$1/4$ teaspoon cinnamon
$1/8$ teaspoon cloves
Seasoning salt and pepper to taste

Brown the boar meat and onions in the olive oil in a large saucepan. Stir in the garlic after the meat is brown, and then add the broth, reserved tomato juice, and all the remaining ingredients. Bring to a boil, and then reduce the heat and simmer on low for about 30 minutes. Check the Rambo soup for seasoning and serve hot.

Woody Forrest's Mule Deer Soup

A fast and easy deer camp meal

6 tablespoons butter
2 pounds mule deer burger, cut with pork fat
I carrot, diced
I onion, diced
I tablespoon wheat flour
6 cups beef stock
3 egg yolks
2 tablespoons lemon juice
$1/2$ tablespoon paprika
Cayenne pepper to taste

Melt the butter in a large saucepan. Add the mule deer burger, carrots, and onions, and sauté over low heat for about 15 minutes. Stir in flour and simmer until well blended. Gradually stir in the stock, scraping up any bits stuck on the bottom of the pan. Bring to a boil; then lower the heat and simmer on low for about 60 minutes. When ready to serve, remove the soup from the heat. Beat the egg yolks, and then beat the lemon juice into them. Slowly add to the soup. Season the soup with salt, pepper, paprika, and cayenne pepper.

Tim Burr's Wild Ox Stew

5 pounds ox meat, cut into stew-sized pieces
$^1/_2$ tablespoon garlic salt
$^1/_2$ teaspoon ground black pepper
$^1/_4$ cup corn oil
1 large yellow onion, quartered
2 tablespoons flour
2 cups Miller Genuine Draft beer
$^1/_4$ cup tarragon vinegar
4 cups chicken broth
2 bay leaves
$^1/_2$ teaspoon dried thyme
2 tablespoons grated horseradish
2 tablespoons grainy mustard
$^1/_2$ cup fresh lemon juice
$^1/_2$ cup heavy whipping cream
3 medium parsnips, peeled and cut into 1-inch rounds
Boiled potatoes

Pat the ox meat dry with paper towels and sprinkle with salt and pepper. Heat the corn oil in a soup pot over medium-high heat on top of the cabin stove. Add the ox meat, without crowding, and brown well on all sides. (Sometimes I have to brown the meat in batches.) Remove the pieces to a plate as they brown. Pour off all but about 2 tablespoons of fat. Reduce the heat to low and replace the pot on the stove. Add the onions and simmer for about 5 minutes, scraping up any brown bits that cling to the pot. Add the flour and sauté for about 1 minute, stirring often. Add the Miller beer, vinegar, and broth, and bring to a boil. Return the meat to the pot with any juices on the plate, and add the bay leaves and thyme. Cover tightly with a lid and simmer on low heat for about 2 hours, or until the ox meat is very tender. Add the remaining ingredients, except the boiled potatoes, and simmer for another 30 minutes, stirring often with a wooden spoon. Check this stew for seasoning and serve hot over boiled potatoes.

Cousin Rick O'Shea's Wild Game Supper Goulash

The leftovers just taste better and better each time you try it.

6 thick slices hickory smoked bacon, diced
I cup elk stew meat, cut into 1-inch cubes
I pound buffalo stew meat, cut into 1-inch cubes
I pound bear meat, cut into 1-inch cubes
2 tablespoons unsalted butter
2 onions, chopped
I garlic clove, minced
I cup all-purpose flour
I teaspoon caraway seeds
3 tablespoons Hungarian sweet paprika
2 teaspoons red pepper flakes
I cup red wine vinegar
2 cups diced tomatoes with juice
5 cups beef stock
12 ounces Coors beer
$^1/_2$ tablespoon seasoned salt
3 cups water
2 red bell peppers, chopped
3 potatoes, peeled and cubed
I parsnip, chopped
3 stalks celery, chopped
4 carrots, chopped
I cup dry seasoned breadcrumbs
$^1/_2$ medium head cabbage, chopped
I cup sweet peas

In a large heavy skillet over medium high heat, fry the bacon for about 10 minutes, or until well browned. Using a slotted spoon, remove the bacon from the skillet and set aide. In small batches, sauté the meats in the bacon fat until all are browned. Use a slotted spoon and set the stew meats aside as well.

Melt the butter in the bacon fat in the same skillet over medium heat. Add the onions and garlic, and sauté for about 5 minutes. Stir in the flour, caraway seeds, paprika, and red pepper flakes. Stir for about 3 minutes until all the flour is dissolved. Whisk in the vinegar and tomatoes. (This mixture should be very thick.) Pour in the beef stock, Coors beer, salt, water, red bell peppers, reserved bacon, and reserved stew meats. Bring to a boil, reduce the heat to low, cover, and simmer for about 60 minutes. Stir in the potatoes, parsnips, celery, and carrots, and continue to simmer, covered, for about 45 minutes, or until all the vegetables are tender. Stir in the breadcrumbs until the stew is thickened. Add the cabbage and peas and simmer for another 5 minutes or so.

Rose Brush's Elk & Bear Meat Stew

2 cups canned tomatoes, diced with juices
I cup beer
3 tablespoons quick-cooking tapioca
2 teaspoons sugar
I teaspoon seasoning salt
$^1/_2$ teaspoon lemon pepper
I pound lean elk meat, cubed
I pound lean bear meat, cubed
3 medium potatoes, peeled and quartered
2 celery ribs, chopped
I red sweet onion, chopped
I slice bead, cubed

In a large bowl, combine the tomatoes, beer, tapioca, sugar, seasoning salt, and pepper. Add the remaining ingredients and mix well. Pour into a greased 3-quart baking dish. Cover and bake at 375 degrees for about 2 hours, or until the elk and bear are tender. Check the stew for seasoning before serving.

Camp Chef Dutch-Oven End-of-Camp Stew

2 pounds elk stew meat, trimmed of fat

1 tablespoon olive oil

12 fresh tomatoes, peeled and cut up

2 cups vegetable juice

3 medium onions, chopped

2 garlic cloves, minced

1/2 teaspoon lemon pepper

2 teaspoons seasoned salt

6 medium potatoes, peeled and quartered

4 carrots, sliced

2 cups corn

2 cups fresh green beans

2 cups peas

3 celery stalks, chopped

1 cup summer squash, sliced

1 cup fresh parsley, snipped

In a Dutch oven, brown the elk meat in oil over medium-high heat. Add the tomatoes, vegetable juice, onions, garlic, lemon pepper, and seasoned salt. Bring to a boil, reduce the heat, and simmer for about 60 minutes. Add the potatoes, carrots, corn, green beans, peas, and celery. Cover and simmer for about 45 minutes. Add the summer squash and simmer for another 45 minutes. Add the parsley, stir, and serve.

Deer Cabin Quick and Easy Vittles

*This is a great-tasting stew that I have every year. After I cook
my deer burger, I place it in a large zip-top bag so it's
ready to use at camp.*

1 medium onion, chopped
2 cans sliced potatoes, drained
2 cans diced tomatoes
1 can cream-style corn
2 pounds deer burger, cooked
$^1/_4$ cup soy sauce
2 tablespoons Worcestershire sauce
1 teaspoon pepper
1 teaspoon hot sauce

After the hunt, stir together all the ingredients in a large Dutch
oven; bring to a boil. Reduce the heat, partially cover, and simmer,
stirring often, for about 60 minutes. This stew is very good served
over cottage-fried potatoes.

Mrs. Shirley Black's "Like a Herd of Buffalo" Stew

This is an old recipe from my mom's side of the family. Rumor is that this recipe has been used for generations, going way back to the old west when my great-grand pappy hunted for hides after the Civil War. This recipe was written originally as a Dutch-oven cooking method.

Large hunk buffalo meat *(about 3 pounds)*
About 3 big spoons of flour *(3 tablespoons)*
1 big spoon bacon fat, or clean fat from critter *(1 tablespoon)*
1 large tin tomatoes *(canned tomatoes, diced)*
2 onions, cut up *(sliced)*
Salt *(1 teaspoon)*
Pepper if ya got it *(1/4 teaspoon black pepper)*
Apple squeezins *($^1/_3$ cup cider vinegar)*
Almost a tin molasses *($^1/_3$ cup molasses)*
1 cup water
Vegetables/roots *(6 carrots, chopped)*
Dried grapes *($^1/_2$ cup raisins)*
Seasonings *($^1/_2$ teaspoon ginger)*

Coat the meat with flour and brown in fat. Add the tin of tomatoes, onions, and seasonings if ya got 'em. Cover the oven and cook fer about 2 hours or more, makin' sure the critter meat's cooked. Add everything else to the dang oven and cook it some more until everything is done. Don't get in a fired-up hurry and burn the vittles. Keep your coals low. Make sure you keep a look-see fer redskins if'n yer cookin where ya ain't supposed to being. Put this stew on top of biscuits if'n ya got 'em.

CHAPTER FOUR

SOUPS AND STEWS USING GAME BIRDS

We're getting happier than a wood tick on a polecat in this chapter! Take it from your old cousin Rick, when hunting game birds there are a few things to remember: Be ready for the hunt! Remember to bring a sharp hunting knife, a steel or whetstone, light rope, plastic bags, paper towels, and a big cooler chock full of clean ice.

Make it a point to field-dress the birds as soon as possible and do the following after the kill:

- Remove the entrails and crop as soon as possible. Remember that the grain in the crop might ferment if not removed soon.
- If you are going to save the heart and liver for giblets, store them in a clean plastic baggie and keep them on ice.
- Cool the carcass as soon as possible to retain the great flavor and maintain the quality of the meat. Never let the carcass reach a temperature above 40 degrees.
- Clean the cavity of the bird with a clean paper towel.
- Allow air to circulate around the carcass by hanging or laying the bird in a well-ventilated place.

- Don't be like Uncle Bubba and the boys and stack the warm birds in a massive pile. Keep them apart.
- Keep your hands, knife, and cutting board clean using hot soapy water, and rinse all thoroughly with cool clean water.
- When cleaning your ducks, remove the wings by cutting them off at the joints, remove the head, and pluck out the pinfeathers. I have learned that feathers may be removed by scalding the birds in hot water (around 140 degrees). The pinfeathers and down can be removed by dipping the feathered bird in a paraffin wax/hot water mixture. When the wax gets hard, the feathers can be scraped off easily.
- When I'm preparing upland birds, such as pheasant, quail, grouse, and partridge, I skin or pluck the bird and soak it in ice-cold water for about 2 hours to remove any excess blood.

This chapter has my favorite soup and stew recipes using wild duck, goose, guinea fowl, pheasant, quail, and squab. I love cooking with game birds, and even though some of the best-tasting recipes (in my opinion) are cooked on a grill, the meat and flavor they produce are also very good in a hot bowl of soup or stew. So Spanky, run out to your freezer (you know, the old one that makes noise in the garage), grab a couple packs of that bird, and let's get ready for some great-tasting vittles!

Calhoun's Wild Turkey Soup

I large yellow onion, chopped

$^1/_2$ cup celery, diced

$^1/_4$ cup butter

2 sweet potatoes, peeled and chopped

3 medium zucchini, chopped

I bunch broccoli, chopped

2 quarts chicken or turkey stock

3 potatoes, diced

2 teaspoons salt

$^1/_2$ teaspoon cayenne

I teaspoon white pepper

2 cups grilled turkey breast, diced

2 cups light cream

In Dutch oven, sauté the onion and celery in butter. Add the sweet potatoes, zucchini, and broccoli; sauté for about 8 minutes, or until just tender. Stir in the stock and simmer for about 10 minutes. Add the potatoes and season to taste. Cook for about 15 minutes and add the grilled wild turkey meat. Stir in the cream and simmer until bubbly. Check for seasoning and serve hot. Note: I use my Holland Legacy Grill for grilling my turkey breast. It takes about 35 minutes, lid closed, turning once at 350 degrees. Other grills may vary in time. Always season meat before grilling.

General Hugh Mercer's Turkey Bird Soup

1 large white onion, chopped

3 ribs celery with leaves, diced

6 tablespoons butter

6 tablespoons flour

1 teaspoon Accent

$1/4$ teaspoon pepper

$1/4$ teaspoon garlic powder with parsley

$1/2$ teaspoon dried thyme

$1/2$ teaspoon savory

$1/2$ teaspoon parsley

2 cups whole milk

5 cups wild turkey meat, cooked and cubed

6 carrots, diced

2 cups chicken broth

10 ounces frozen peas

In a large soup kettle, sauté the onion and celery in butter until tender. Stir in the flour and seasonings and gradually add the whole milk, stirring constantly, until thickened. Add the turkey meat and carrots. Add just enough broth so that the soup is at the desired consistency. Cover and simmer on low heat for about 30 minutes. Add the peas; cover and simmer for another 20 minutes, or until the vegetables are tender. Check the soup for seasoning and serve hot.

Iowa Long Spurs Soup

5 cups chicken stock
I teaspoon dried thyme, crushed
$^1/_2$ teaspoon fresh black pepper
I cup packaged dried shell macaroni
16 ounces frozen mixed vegetables
2 cups chopped wild turkey meat, cooked
$^3/_4$ cup frozen orange juice

In a large saucepan, combine the stock, thyme, and pepper. Bring to a boil. Stir in the macaroni shells and return to boiling; reduce heat. Boil gently, uncovered, for about 3 minutes. Stir in the vegetables and return to a boil. Boil gently, uncovered, for about 8 more minutes, or until the vegetables and pasta are tender. Stir in the wild turkey meat and thawed orange juice. Heat through. Check the soup for seasoning and serve hot.

Camp Chef Dutch-Oven Pheasant Soup

5 cups cabbage, finely chopped
3 carrots, finely sliced
I cup celery, chopped
I quart spicy vegetable juice
2 cups chicken broth
$^1/_2$ teaspoon pepper
I onion, finely chopped
About 3 pounds pheasant breast, skinned and boned, cut into
   bite-sized pieces
I teaspoon sweet paprika
$^1/_4$ cup white wine

Add all the vegetables along with the broth, seasonings (except paprika), and juice to the Dutch oven. Bring the mixture to a boil; then cover and simmer for about 45 minutes. In a skillet, brown the pheasant meat over medium heat, covering each side with sweet paprika. Continue to brown and turn until the meat is done through and no longer pink. Deglaze the skillet with the white wine. Cut the pheasant meat into cubes, and add it to cabbage broth, along with juices from the skillet. Cover the Dutch oven, and continue to simmer for about 60 minutes. Check the soup for seasoning and serve hot.

Harpers Ferry Pheasant Chowder

About 5 pounds pheasant breast
3 stalks celery
^{1}/$_2$ teaspoon parsley
4 quarts chicken stock
I tablespoon salt
^{1}/$_2$ cup barley, uncooked
^{1}/$_2$ pound bacon, cooked and crumbled
2 large carrots, sliced
I cup frozen corn
I cup frozen peas
I can evaporated milk
2 large potatoes, cubed
White pepper to taste

In a large pot, combine all the ingredients together and simmer on low heat until the pheasant breasts are tender. Slowly and carefully allow the meat to cool. Shred the meat into bite-sized pieces and add back to soup. Simmer on low for about 30 minutes, check for seasoning, and serve hot. Very good over buttermilk biscuits.

Wings-a-Flappin' Soup

1 cup wild rice
4¹/₂ cups chicken broth
¹/₂ teaspoon pepper
2 cups fresh mushrooms, sliced
¹/₂ cup shallots, chopped
2 tablespoons butter
2 cups cooked duck breasts, chopped
¹/₂ cup fresh parsley, snipped

Run cold water over the wild rice in a strainer for about 1 minute, lifting rice to rinse it thoroughly. In a large saucepan, mix the wild rice, broth, and pepper. Bring to a boil; reduce heat. Cover and simmer for about 60 minutes, or until the rice is tender. Meanwhile, in a cast-iron skillet, cook the mushrooms and shallots in butter until all are tender but not brown. Add the mushroom mixture, duck meat, and parsley to soup. Simmer on low for about 20 minutes and serve hot after checking for seasoning.

Mill Creek Quail and Sausage Gumbo

2 pounds quail meat
2 tablespoons flour
Salt and pepper to taste
16 ounces sausage, smoked link
1 large fresh tomato
1 large onion, chopped
2 pounds fresh okra
2 tablespoons oil
3 quarts chicken stock

Cut up the quail meat and dredge it in flour seasoned with salt and pepper. Fry the meat in a large cast-iron skillet until brown. Slice up the sausage. After the quail is browned, place the sausage in the same skillet. Brown the sausage on all sides. Save the fat from the quail and sausage meat. Fry the tomato, onions, and okra in about 2 tablespoons oil, until all are tender. Make a roux with 2 teaspoons oil and 2 teaspoons flour, stir, and brown over low heat until the roux is as dark as possible without burning it. Place the quail and sausage in the roux and stir well. Place all the ingredients into a heavy, deep iron pan, add the stock and cook for about 2 hours on low heat. After the gumbo has thickened, check for seasoning and serve.

Nutter Fort Turkey Corn Chowder

4 pounds wild turkey wings (checked for shot)
8 cups cold chicken broth
1 teaspoon salt
12 ounces frozen sweet corn
$^1/_2$ teaspoon black pepper
$^1/_4$ cup parsley, chopped fine

Place the turkey wings, broth, and salt in a large soup kettle. Bring to a rolling boil, and remove any froth that gathers on top. Reduce the heat to a simmer and cook for about 2 hours. Strain the soup and allow the turkey wings to cool. Remove the meat from the bones, and discard the bones and skin. Return the meat to the broth and again place over the heat. Bring to a simmer and add the corn and black pepper. Cook for about 20 minutes longer. Stir in the chopped parsley just before serving. Serve over Vista Bakery oyster crackers.

Rum Creek County Hunters Squab Soup

1 pound squab breasts, skinned, deboned, and chopped
1 tablespoon olive oil
6 cups chicken stock
2 tablespoons chicken bouillon
2 cups broccoli florets
2 cups carrots, peeled and sliced
3/4 cup red bell pepper, chopped
Salt and pepper to taste

In a large Dutch oven, brown the squab meat in olive oil. Add the remaining ingredients and bring to a boil. Reduce the coals (heat) and simmer uncovered for about 60 minutes, stirring occasionally. Check the soup for seasoning and serve hot from the Dutch oven.

Carol Kuntz, Cousin Rick's Biggest Fan, Guinea Fowl Soup

About 5 pounds guinea breast meat, cut up
2 teaspoons garlic salt
1/2 teaspoon saffron
2 cups frozen corn
2 cups egg noodles
1 tablespoon parsley, chopped
2 eggs, hard cooked
Black pepper to taste

Cover the meat with 3 quarts water and bring to a boil. Skim, turn down the heat to low, add the salt and saffron, and steep until the meat is tender. Remove the meat and strain the stock. Take the guinea meat from the bone and return to the stock. Add the corn and bring to a boil. Add the egg noodles and cook until the noodles are tender. Add the parsley, eggs, and pepper and serve hot.

John and Shaena's Squab Chowder

3 pounds squab, cut up
4 cups chicken stock
I large yellow onion, chopped
I teaspoon poultry seasoning
I 16-ounce can corn, with liquid
I 16-ounce can whole tomatoes, drained and chopped
I teaspoon lemon juice
Salt and pepper to taste

In a large saucepan, simmer the squab in chicken stock, onion, and poultry seasoning for about 60 minutes. Remove the squab and let cool; reserve the broth. Skim the fat from the broth. Remove the meat from the squab; discard the skin and bones. Chop the meat into bite-sized pieces. In a large non-aluminum saucepan, combine the squab, broth, corn, tomatoes, and lemon juice. Simmer for about 45 minutes. Season with salt and pepper and serve hot.

Smokin' Gun's Quail Soup

3 quail
I tablespoon butter
I tablespoon bacon fat
2 carrots, sliced
I onion, sliced
I cup peas, shelled
4 large mushroom caps, sliced
2 tablespoons flour
I teaspoon parsley, flat, chopped
$^1/_4$ teaspoon seasoned salt
6 cups chicken stock
$^1/_4$ cup sour cream

Clean the quail and cut into serving pieces. Melt the butter and fat in a large soup pot. Brown the quail very rapidly until well browned. Add the vegetables, mushrooms, and about $^1/_2$ cup water. Cook slowly, uncovered, until the water almost disappears. Add the flour, parsley, and salt; stir well. Add the chicken stock and bring to a boil. Simmer on low heat for another 60 minutes. Just before serving, mix in the sour cream and serve hot over dumplings.

SCALDING YOUR GAME BIRDS

Birds can be scalded by dipping them in hot water (around 145 degrees or so). This relaxes the muscle tissue around each feather so the feathers can be removed easily. However, if the birds are held for several hours or frozen before plucking, then scalding may break down the fatty tissue in the skin, resulting in difficult plucking and skin tears. This, of course, will put you down nine miles of ugly road! Some game birds pluck easier than others. Immature birds will generally have pinfeathers, especially early in the season, and more tender skin. If you want to serve the birds whole, I would recommend you pick them. One general rule may be to pluck the larger, more perfect birds and skin those that are smaller or have a lot of shot.

The large tendons that run up into the shank can be removed easily at this time if you haven't removed the feet.

Cut through the skin of the leg $1^1/_2$ inches above the hock joint. Do not cut the tendons. I always lay the bird at the edge of a table with the cut just above the table edge. The leg should project over the table edge. Press the leg down sharply with the side of your hand. The bone should snap at the joint. Tendons should come away with the foot. If they tear away from the feet, remove one by one with a skewer or a large pair of tweezers. Fishy-tasting ducks or those that feed on aquatic vegetation and animals probably should be skinned.

Lab-in-the-Truck Cheesy Goose Chowder

3 cups chicken broth
2 cups diced peeled potatoes
I cup diced carrots
I cup diced celery
$^1/_2$ cup diced white onions
I teaspoon seasoned salt
$^1/_2$ teaspoon lemon pepper
$^1/_4$ cup butter
$^1/_3$ cup flour
2 cups milk
2 cups shredded cheddar cheese
2 cups diced cooked goose meat

In a medium-sized saucepan, bring the chicken broth to a boil. Reduce the heat; add the potatoes, carrots, celery, onion, salt, and pepper. Cover and simmer for about 20 minutes, or until the vegetables are tender. Meanwhile, melt the butter in a saucepan; add the flour and mix well. Gradually stir in the milk; simmer over low heat until slightly thickened. Stir in the cheese and simmer until melted; add the broth with the goose meat. Simmer and stir over low heat until heated through.

Ring Eye Duck and Chili Soup Vittles

1 tablespoon butter
1 cup onion, finely chopped
1 garlic clove, minced
1 large celery stalk, diced
5 cups chicken stock
1 cup boneless duck breasts, chopped and cooked
$1/2$ cup green canned chiles
2 cups cauliflower florets, chopped
1 cup canned kidney beans, drained of juice
2 tablespoons cornstarch
$1/4$ cup cold Miller Lite beer
1 cup sharp Cheddar cheese or Colby Jack

In a large soup kettle, melt the butter over medium heat. Add the onion, garlic, celery, stock, cooked duck meat, chiles, cauliflower, and kidney beans. Meanwhile, in a small mixing bowl or cup, combine the cornstarch and cold beer. Add this mixture in 2 separate batches to the soup, stirring well after each batch. Add the cheese to the soup. Check the soup for seasoning and serve hot or keep in the refrigerator for up to 3 days to serve in the blind.

Wild Bill Elliot's Wild Turkey and Ham Soup

1 wild turkey breast fillet, grilled about 45 minutes, turning once, skinned and sliced thinly
2 ounces mushrooms, sliced
2 ounces smoked ham, chopped
2 large yellow onions, chopped
1 pint chicken stock
2 teaspoons soy sauce
1 teaspoon corn flour
Holland Grill Seasoning to taste

Place the turkey slices, mushrooms, ham, onions, and stock in a Dutch oven. Bring to a boil. Reduce the heat and simmer uncovered for about 30 minutes. Blend the soy sauce with the corn flour and add to the oven, stirring constantly until the soup thickens. Season with Holland Grill seasoning and serve immediately from Dutch oven.

Chad Cooper's Goose Blind Surprise

6 cups strong flavor chicken stock
2 tablespoons olive oil
1/2 cup chopped carrots
1/2 cup chopped celery
1/2 cup chopped red onion
1/2 cup chopped zucchini
1/2 cup chopped yellow squash
1 cup cooked wild rice
2 cups cooked goose meat, shredded
Garlic salt and black pepper to taste
4 sprigs of chopped cilantro

Bring the stock to a boil in a large pot. In a separate large pot, heat the oil and sauté the carrots, celery, onion, zucchini, and yellow squash. Add the boiling stock to the vegetables, and then stir in the rice and cooked goose meat. Season with garlic salt and pepper to taste. Simmer the soup for about 30 minutes and ladle into bowls topped with chopped cilantro.

Mark and Rita Carlson's Iowa Pheasants Soup

2 pheasants, quartered
Salt and pepper to taste
2 tablespoons butter
4 leeks, sliced
2 Granny Smith apples, peeled
1 cup apple wine
$^1/_2$ cup cider vinegar
3 cups chicken stock
3 tablespoons Calvados
$^1/_2$ cup heavy cream

Season the pheasants with salt and pepper. Melt the butter over medium heat in a saucepan just large enough to hold the pheasants. Add the pheasant meat, skin side down, and cook for about 10 minutes. If the butter in the pan starts to brown, lower the heat slightly. Turn the meat and lightly sauté in the same way for about 5 minutes more. Remove the meat from the pan and place it in a large bowl. If the butter in the pan has burned, pour it out and replace it with two tablespoons of fresh butter. Add the leeks and sauté them for about 10 minutes over medium heat. Stir the leeks every couple of minutes. The leeks should be tender but not brown. Place the pheasant meat back into the pan with the cooked leeks. Add the apples, wine, vinegar, and broth. Bring the liquids to a slow simmer and with a ladle, skim off any fat or froth that floats to the top. Cover the pot and simmer the pheasants very gently for about 15 minutes, until they are completely cooked. Remove the pheasants and let the meat cool. Cut the meat into bite-sized pieces. Use a ladle to skim off any fat that has formed on the surface of the liquid in the sauté pan. Add the Calvados and heavy cream. Bring to a low simmer and season to taste with salt and pepper. Heat the chunks of pheasant in the soup for about 5 minutes and serve immediately in hot soup bowls.

Illinois Duffy's Riverbank Gumbo

2 large ducks, cut into 8 pieces
2 teaspoons dried mustard
2 teaspoons sweet paprika
$^1/_4$ teaspoon salt
$^1/_4$ teaspoon fresh pepper
$^1/_8$ teaspoon ground allspice
$^1/_4$ teaspoon cayenne
2 tablespoons olive oil
4 cups okra, fresh or frozen
5 celery stalks, cut into $^1/_2$-inch slices
2 white onions, coarsely chopped
2 red bell peppers, cored and diced
1 green bell pepper, cored and diced
1 tablespoon finely chopped garlic
1 cup canned plum tomatoes, drained (reserve the juice)
2 tablespoons tomato paste
1 teaspoon dried thyme
1 bay leaf
$^1/_4$ cup flat-leaf parsley, chopped
Cooked wild rice

Rinse the duck pieces and pat dry; check for shot. Preheat the oven to 400 degrees. Combine the spices in a small bowl and rub into the duck meat. Place the duck in a shallow baking pan and bake for about 25 minutes. Set the cooked duck aside. Place the oil in a large, heavy pot. Add the okra, celery, onions, red peppers, green peppers, and garlic; cook over low heat, stirring, for about 5 minutes. Add the tomatoes, tomato paste, thyme, and bay leaf. Add the duck meat and any pan juice to the pot. Cover with the reserved tomato juice, making sure that all the duck pieces are covered in liquid. Simmer over medium-low heat, partially covered, until the duck is tender, about 30 minutes. Stir in 2 tablespoons parsley. Cook, uncovered, for about 20 minutes longer. If the gumbo begins to boil, reduce the heat. Adjust the seasonings to taste. Garnish with remaining parsley. Serve the duck gumbo over wild rice.

Green Horn Quail Soup

$^1/_2$ pound boneless quail breast meat
2 cups chicken stock
I cup fresh mushrooms, quartered
4 tablespoons sesame oil
2 tablespoons cooking sherry
2 tablespoons fresh parsley, chopped

Thinly slice the quail breast meat. Bring the chicken stock to a rolling boil and add the quail and mushrooms. When the soup starts to boil again and all of the ingredients start to float to the top, remove from the heat. Add the sesame oil and cooking sherry and taste for seasoning. Add salt and pepper if needed. Serve in soup bowls and sprinkle with chopped parsley.

Lake Blue Grass Duck

6 dried Chinese mushrooms
2 quarts chicken stock
$^1/_4$ teaspoon white pepper
I cup Chinese greens
Bones from one roasted duck
4 green onions, chopped
I teaspoon sesame oil
I cup cooked duck meat, chopped
I ounce egg noodles
Salt and pepper to taste
I large egg, raw
I tablespoon parsley, chopped

Soak the dried mushrooms in about 1 cup warm water for about 30 minutes. Bring the chicken stock to a simmer and add the mushrooms and water in which they were soaked. Add the pepper, greens, and wild duck bones. Simmer stock for about 60 minutes. Drain the stock and discard all the solids except the mushrooms. Cut the mushrooms and return to the stockpot. Add the greens, onions, sesame oil, and cooked duck meat. Check for seasoning, and add salt and pepper if needed. Add the egg noodles to the pot and simmer until they are just tender, about 8 minutes. Place the soup in a tureen and add the raw egg, whole. Add the parsley garnish. Stir the egg into the soup at the cabin table. Serve hot.

Camp Chef Pheasant Soup

2 tablespoons olive oil
2 tablespoons unsalted butter
3 carrots cut into $^1/_2$-inch slices
4 celery stalks, chopped
1 parsnip, peeled and minced
2 cloves garlic, diced
4 cups chicken stock
3 cups canned plum tomatoes, drained and crushed
1 cup lentils, rinsed
2 pounds pheasant, quartered
8 tablespoons Italian parsley
1 tablespoon rosemary, chopped
$^1/_4$ teaspoon allspice, ground
$^3/_4$ cup dry sherry
Salt and pepper to taste

Heat the oil and butter in a Dutch oven. Add the carrots, onions, celery, parsnip, and garlic. Cook, covered, over medium heat for about 20 minutes, or until just tender. Add the stock, tomatoes, lentils, and pheasant pieces, and simmer, partially covered, for about 20 minutes. Add the remaining ingredients, stir, and simmer for about 30 minutes with the Dutch-oven lid on. Remove the pheasant meat, and allow the meat to cool. Remove all the meat from the bones and add it back to the Dutch oven. Continue to simmer on low coals until ready to serve.

Granny Black's Green Island Squab & Pepper Soup

2 pounds squab breasts, skinned and deboned
2 large red bell peppers, roasted
1 medium onion, chopped
2 cups chicken broth
2 tablespoons lime juice
1 tablespoon cilantro, chopped fresh
1/2 teaspoon seasoned salt
1/2 teaspoon lemon pepper
2 garlic cloves, crushed
1 cup jicama, cubed (Mexican turnip)

Set the oven to broil. Place the squab breast on a rack in the broiler pan. Place the broiler pan so the top of the squab is about 7 inches from heat. Broil the meat for about 20 minutes, turning once, until done. Cut the meat into 1/4-inch strips. Place the peppers and onion in blender. Cover and blend until smooth. Heat the pepper and onion mixture, broth, lime juice, cilantro, seasoned salt, pepper, and garlic to boiling in a medium saucepan; reduce the heat. Simmer for about 20 minutes. Stir in the cooked squab meat and jicama. Simmer on low for about 15 minutes and serve hot.

Skeeter in My Eye Snow Goose Soup

5 cups thin coconut milk
1 pound goose breast meat, sliced
3 stalks lemon grass, bruised and chopped
2 teaspoon Laos powder
5 green onions, finely chopped
2 tablespoons coriander leaves, chopped

In a large saucepan, bring the milk to a boil. Add the goose meat pieces, lemon grass, and Laos powder. Reduce the heat and simmer until the goose meat is tender, about 20 minutes. Do not cover, as this will cause the milk to curdle. When the meat is good and tender, add the green onions and coriander leaves. Bring the heat up just below boiling. Check the soup for seasoning and serve hot in warm bowls.

KEEP YOUR CAMP KITCHEN CLEAN AND SAFE!

Like other high-protein foods, wild game birds must be handled carefully in the camp kitchen. Bacteria and other microorganisms can easily be spread through a kitchen by unwashed hands, equipment, or mishandled food. To reduce risk of foodborne illness, follow Cousin Rick's kitchen camp food safety rules:

Wash your paws! Wash your hands for at least 30 seconds with hot soap and water before beginning to work and after changing tasks or after doing anything that could contaminate your hands, such as sneezing or using the latrine.

Start off clean. Start with clean equipment. After using it, clean it thoroughly with hot soapy water, rinse well, and sanitize with a solution of 1 tablespoon chlorine bleach per gallon of water (or approximately 1 teaspoon per four cups water). After spraying the surface or dipping cutting boards in the solution, allow to air dry. Remake sanitizing solution daily.

Thaw it safely. Thaw frozen meat in a refrigerator at 40 degrees or below on the lowest shelf to make sure blood and juices don't drip on ready-to-eat foods. Meat also may be safely thawed in a microwave (immediately followed by cooking), sealed in a plastic bag and placed under cold running water, or as part of the cooking process.

Two boards are better than one. Use separate cutting boards for cutting up raw meat and ready-to-eat foods like salad ingredients and bread.

Meat thermometers rule! Use a food thermometer to measure doneness of game meat. For safety, cook game meats and game birds to an internal temperature of at least 165 degrees.

Cool it, Bubba! Promptly refrigerate leftover cooked meat in shallow pans. Use all cooked game meat within two to three days, no longer.

Keep in mind that plucked game birds can be roasted without fear of drying them out because the fat beneath the skin will be absorbed into the meat. However, if the birds are skinned, wrap them with bacon, dredge with flour, or put them in oven bags to prevent the bird from drying out while cooking. Another Cousin Rick trick is to dip a slice of bread in egg and milk and place it on the surface of the bird while roasting. If the bird is to be cut into small soup-sized pieces, test the joints and bones to determine the best cookery method. If the joints are stiff and the bones brittle, the bird is old and should be braised (simmered in a cover pot with a small amount of liquid) or stewed to make it more tender and enjoyable. If the joints are flexible and the bones soft, the bird can be fried. Again always use a food thermometer to gauge the doneness of game birds.

Guinea Fowl Soup Alexander

2 pounds guinea fowl meat
1 cup condensed cream of celery soup
$^1/_4$ cup flour
2 zucchini, chopped
1 teaspoon paprika
$^1/_2$ teaspoon fresh basil
1 garlic clove, minced
1 cup canned tomato wedges, drained

Rinse the guinea fowl meat and pat dry. Mix the celery soup with the flour. Combine all the ingredients into a large crock; stir thoroughly to coat the fowl. Cover and cook on low for about 10 hours.

Ben-Hur Duck Soup

3 pounds wild duck, cut up
I large onion, finely chopped
2 medium carrots, finely chopped
2 cups diced celery
I medium russet potato, peeled and diced
$^1/_4$ cup parsley, chopped
$^1/_4$ cup canned tomato sauce
2 cans chicken broth
I can cream-style corn
2 medium zucchini, chopped
Garlic salt and pepper to taste

Rinse the duck meat, pat dry, and set aside. In a 4-quart or larger slow cooker, combine onions, carrots, celery, potatoes, and 3 tablespoons parsley. Add the duck meat, and then pour in the tomato sauce and broth. Cover and cook at low setting until the duck and potatoes are very tender when pierced, about 8 hours. Lift out the duck and let stand until cool enough to handle. Meanwhile, skim and discard fat from the broth mixture. Stir in the corn to broth mixture; increase cooker heat setting to high. Cover and cook on high for another 20 minutes more. Remove and discard all the bones and skin from the duck meat. Tear the meat into bite-sized shreds. Add the duck meat and zucchini to soup; cover and cook until the zucchini is just tender to bite, about 20 minutes. Season to taste with garlic salt and pepper. Sprinkle the remaining parsley over all.

Cold Water Goose Camp Soup

2 pounds skinless, boneless goose meat, grilled or roasted
1 large red potato, diced
2 cups frozen corn
1 medium onion, chopped
$^1/_2$ cup chopped celery
3 tablespoons Dijon mustard
$^1/_4$ teaspoon freshly ground black pepper
$^1/_8$ teaspoon garlic juice
3 cups spicy vegetable juice
1 cup chicken stock

Cut the grilled or roasted goose meat into bite-sized pieces. Combine all ingredients, including the goose meat, in a large slow cooker. Stir well and check for seasoning. Cover and cook on low heat for about 10 hours or on high heat for about 5 hours.

Fort Clark Springs Wild Gobbler Bone Soup

I first tried this outstanding soup at spring turkey camp in 2002. Several other ingredients are great in this soup, so play around and develop your own gobbler bone soup!

Large turkey carcass, including all bones and neck
3 quarts water (or chicken stock)
3 cups celery, thinly sliced
1 cup onion, diced
Seasoned salt and fresh black pepper to taste
1 cup quick-cooking long rice

Place the gobbler carcass in a large pot. Add water (or broth), celery, onion, and seasonings. Cover and simmer on low for about 8 hours. Strain mixture with colander. Return broth to pot and increase heat to medium. Remove all meat from the gobbler bones. Puree the vegetables in a food processor or blender. Add the puree, meat, and rice to the broth in pot. Cover the pot and simmer for about 60 minutes, or until all ingredients are warm and tender.

Gun Barrel City Squab Stew

1 pound squab cuts, chopped into stew-sized pieces
Sliced carrots
Sliced celery
Thinly sliced onions
3 large potatoes, peeled and cut into bite-sized pieces
Chicken broth to cover (or use 5 chicken bouillon cubes)
Dried parsley
2 tablespoons soy sauce
Frank's Red Hot Sauce to taste
Pennsylvania Dutch noodles

Combine all the ingredients in a large slow cooker. Cook on high for about 4 hours or on low for about 8 hours until all is tender and done. Add as many vegetables and seasonings as desired.

Amana Colonies Pheasant & Corn Soup

3 pounds pheasant
2 quarts chicken stock or broth
$^1/_2$ cup onion, coarsely chopped
$^1/_2$ cup carrots, coarsely chopped
$^1/_2$ cup celery, coarsely chopped
1 teaspoon saffron threads
1 cup corn kernels, fresh or frozen
1 tablespoon fresh parsley, chopped
1 cup egg noodles, cooked
Seasonings to taste

Combine the pheasant with chicken stock, chopped onions, carrots, celery, and saffron threads. Bring the stock to a simmer. Simmer for about 60 minutes, skimming the surface as necessary. Remove and reserve the stewing pheasants until cool enough to handle; then pick the meat from the bones. Cut the meat into neat little pieces. Strain the saffron from the broth through a fine sieve. Add all ingredients to broth and return to a rapid boil. Cook until all is tender and hot.

Hillsboro Chunky Squab Soup

1 large onion, chopped
3 celery stalks, thinly sliced
2 large carrots, peeled and thinly sliced
2 cups cauliflower florets
4 thick squab breasts halves
6 cups chicken stock, defatted
2 cups garbanzo beans, cooked
$1/2$ cup long-grain rice, uncooked
1 teaspoon dried thyme leaves
1 teaspoon dried basil leaves
1 teaspoon dried marjoram leaves
2 large bay leaves
$1/2$ teaspoon white pepper
2 cups stewed tomatoes

In a large slow cooker, combine the onions, celery, carrots, and cauliflower. Add the squab breasts, stock, beans, rice, thyme, basil, marjoram, bay leaves, and pepper. Cover and cook on high setting for about 60 minutes. Lower heat to low and cook an additional 6 to 8 hours. Remove the bay leaves and discard. Remove the squab. When cool enough to handle, remove the meat from the bone and cut into bite-sized pieces. Add the stewed tomatoes to the slow cooker, and cook an additional 20 minutes. Return the squab meat to slow cooker, and cook an additional 10 minutes.

Old Glory Hot Wild Turkey Soup

6 cups milk
3 $10^{3}/4$-ounce cans condensed cream of chicken soup, undiluted
3 cups shredded cooked wild turkey breast meat (about 1 pound)
1 cup sour cream (about 8 ounces)
$1/2$ cup hot sauce (I use Frank's Red Hot)

Combine all the ingredients in a slow cooker. Cover and cook on low heat for about 5 hours. The last time I had this great soup, a good hunting buddy of mine garnished it with jalapeño peppers. We were well into the beers and it tasted great!

Gray Wing Ranch Wild Turkey Giblet Soup

Uncooked giblets of 1 or 2 big toms
6 cups cold water
Salt to taste
Fresh ground pepper to taste
³/₄ cup carrots, finely diced
³/₄ cup onion, chopped
³/₄ cup celery, including the leaves, finely chopped
10 ounces spicy bloody Mary mix
1 tablespoon parsley, minced
1 teaspoon minced garlic
1 teaspoon paprika
3 tablespoons quick-cooking oatmeal

Wash the giblets with ice-cold water and discard any fat. Place the cleaned giblets in a large cooking pot with water and salt. Bring to a boil and simmer for about 30 minutes. Add the remaining ingredients except the oatmeal; simmer soup gently about 30 minutes more. Remove the wild turkey giblets and chop into small pieces. Return the chopped giblets to the soup; add the oatmeal, stir, and simmer on low heat for another 15 minutes. Check the soup for seasoning and serve hot in warm bowls.

Three Rivers Wild Boar & Duck Chowder

6 cups chicken stock
2 cups cooked boar meat, diced
2 cups cooked duck breast meat, cubed
2 cups potatoes, cubed
8 small onions, quartered
I cup corn, canned or fresh
I cup cut green beans
I cup lima beans
I cup canned tomatoes
2 stalks celery with leaves, chopped
I tablespoon parsley, minced
I teaspoon seasoned salt
$^1/_2$ teaspoon white pepper
I bay leaf

Combine all the ingredients in a slow cooker. Cover and cook on low for 6 to 8 hours, or on high 3 to 4 hours. Serve in heated soup bowls garnished with chopped fresh parsley.

Winchester Soup

2 cups canned tomatoes, cut up, with juices
2 cups diced cooked goose meat
$^1/_2$ cup sliced carrots
$^1/_2$ cup sliced celery
$^1/_4$ cup sliced canned mushrooms, drained
3 teaspoons instant chicken bouillon granules
I bay leaf
$^1/_4$ teaspoon dried thyme, crushed
5 cups water
I cup cooked medium noodles
Salt and pepper to taste

In slow cooker, combine tomatoes, cooked goose meat, carrots, celery, mushrooms, bouillon, bay leaf, and thyme. Stir in water. Cover and cook on low for 6 to 8 hours. Turn to high; stir in cooked noodles. Cover and heat through, about 15 minutes. Stir well and remove bay leaf. Check the soup for seasoning and serve hot.

MIDWEST HUNTERS FUN!

I know I shouldn't do it, but my mouth has always written checks my rumpus can't cash!

Three pheasant hunters are sitting around a campfire: one was from Missouri, the second was from Wisconsin, and the last hunter was from Iowa. The hunter from Missouri opens up a bottle of Budweiser, takes a swig, then throws the bottle in the air, pulls out a double-barreled shotgun, and blasts the bottle to pieces.

The hunter from Iowa says, "Why didn't you finish it"? The hunter from Missouri replies, "It's okay, we've got plenty of Budweiser where I come from." The hunter from Wisconsin then pulls out a bottle of Miller, takes a sip, then throws the bottle in the air, and blasts it with his shotgun. He looks at the other hunters and says, "That's okay, we've got plenty of Miller in Wisconsin." The Iowa hunter then pulls out a bottle of Big Buck Micro-Brewery Ale, drinks it all down, and then tosses the empty bottle into the air, pulls up his shotgun, shoots the guy from Wisconsin, and then before the bottle hits the ground, he catches it. He looks over at the Missourian and says, "It's okay, we've got plenty of hunters from Wisconsin in Iowa, but we have a five-cent deposit on bottles."

Argo's Guinea Chow

2 uncooked guinea breasts, deboned, skinned, and sliced into thin strips
1 tablespoon egg white, lightly whipped
6 cups chicken broth
$^1/_4$ teaspoon sugar
1 tablespoon soy sauce
1 cucumber, peeled and julienned
$^3/_4$ teaspoon dark sesame oil
Salt and white pepper to taste

Mix the guinea strips into the egg white and set aside. Pour chicken broth, sugar, and soy sauce into a large soup pan, and bring it to a boil. Stir in the meat strips and the cucumber and bring it back to a boil. Stir in the sesame oil, salt, and pepper to taste and serve into warm soup bowls.

Hooch's Tap & Bait Goose Hunters Soup

4 cups chicken broth
2 tablespoons soy sauce
1 tablespoon molasses
2 tablespoons fresh lemon juice
2 cloves garlic, minced
$^1/_4$ cup peanut butter
$^1/_4$ cup peanuts, chopped fine
1 cup cooked goose meat, chopped fine
$^3/_4$ cup green onions, sliced in rings

In a large saucepan, combine the broth, soy sauce, molasses, lemon juice, and garlic. Bring the mixture to a low boil; then reduce heat and simmer, uncovered, for about 20 minutes. Whisk in the peanut butter, and then simmer for about 8 more minutes or so. Just before serving, stir in the peanuts, goose meat, and green onion rings. Heat through and serve in warm bowls.

Renards Mississippi River Cabin Duck Soup

4 cups chicken stock
I cup cooked duck breasts, shredded
I cup cooked wild rice
I cup canned chickpeas, drained
I chipotle pepper, seeded and chopped fine
Oregano to taste
I cup Monterey Jack cheese
I avocado, chopped

Heat the stock in a Dutch oven, then stir in the duck, rice, chickpeas, chipotle pepper, and oregano to taste. Simmer for about 15 minutes, or until all the ingredients are heated through. To serve, ladle into warm bowls and top with cheese and avocado.

Colder Than a Hunter's Butt Soup

2 tablespoons butter
2 tablespoons onion, minced
2 teaspoons curry powder
I tablespoon flour
4 cups chicken broth
4 egg yolks
2 cups whipping cream
$^1/_2$ cup cooked game bird meat, diced

Melt the butter in a large saucepan over medium heat. Add the onion and sauté until translucent. Add the curry and flour. Simmer for about 5 minutes. Add the broth and bring to a boil, whisking until smooth. Whip in the egg yolks and simmer for about 2 minutes. Press through a fine sieve and chill over night. When ready to serve, stir in cold whipping cream and cooked game bird meat. Check the soup for seasoning and serve in ice-cold bowls.

Grillin' Like a Villain Wild Turkey Soup

Grillin' Like a Villain, gotta love this book!

4 cups chopped, grilled wild turkey breast
8 cups chicken stock
2 cups hot salsa
1 cup chopped white onions
2 chicken bouillon cubes
1 cup chopped carrots
1 cup chopped green bell peppers
Chopped parsley to taste
Seasoned salt to taste
Fresh-ground black pepper to taste
1 teaspoon dried basil
Worcestershire sauce to taste
$^2/_3$ cup dried barley, cooked

In a large stockpot, combine the grilled wild turkey, stock, salsa, onions, and bouillon cubes. Bring to a boil, reduce the heat, and simmer for about 2 hours, stirring occasionally. Add the remaining ingredients, except the barley, and simmer until the vegetables are tender. Stir in the barley just before serving.

CHAPTER FIVE

SOUPS AND STEWS USING FISH AND SEAFOOD

Have you ever thought about the fish you catch? I have learned from years of experience that it is clearly best to keep your catch alive as long as possible. You can use a live box or a metal link basket—both are much better than a rusty old stringer! And by all means, don't toss the fish in the bottom of the boat. I use a large ice chest filled with ice to keep my harvest fresh. The sooner the fish are cleaned and cooled, the better they will taste, hands down!

I have gotten into the habit of cutting the throat as I do with all wild game; then I remove the gills and entrails, wipe the surface, and place the fish in plastic bags and on ice. This way I can finish the task of preparation later.

One thing to keep in mind is that the digestive juices of fish are strong. If the fish are not cleaned promptly, they will start to digest the entrails, and that's not a good thing. It causes poor flavors to seep into the meat.

The flesh on the inside of fish gets soft and off-flavored in the rib area. Don't forget about bleeding because the blood quickly breaks down and seeps into the meat. I simply cut the throat and remove the gills in a timely manner.

If you are ice fishing or fishing in the winter months, be sure to keep your fish covered because the wind will dry them out.

Fish can be frozen whole, just as they come out of the water. I simply wrap them in heavy freezer paper, and keep them well frozen.

And then when I'm ready to prepare the fish to eat, I thaw them in cold water and clean as I would when freshly caught.

COUSIN RICK'S SEAFOOD STORAGE TIPS

- Store your fresh seafood in the coldest part of your refrigerator. I usually use the lowest shelf at the back or in the meat keeper.
- Don't suffocate live lobsters, oysters, clams, or mussels by sealing them in plastic bags. They need to breathe, so always store them covered with a clean damp cloth. Before cooking, check that the lobsters are moving. Make sure the clams and mussels are still alive by tapping open shells. Discard any that do not close.
- Keep raw and cooked seafood separate to prevent bacterial cross-contamination. After handling raw seafood, thoroughly wash knives, cutting surfaces, sponges, and your hands with hot soapy water.

Reely Mine Crab Soup

2 cups diced red onions
3 tablespoons melted butter
30 ounces dark beef stock
6 cups water
$1/4$ cup leeks, chopped
3 tablespoons Old Bay seasoning
I large tomato, chopped
$1/4$ pound string beans
2 stalks celery, chopped
8 ounces corn
6 carrots, sliced
6 potatoes, sliced
I pound crabmeat, chopped

In a large soup pot, sauté the onions in butter until tender. Add the remaining ingredients except the crabmeat and simmer for about 2 hours. Add the crabmeat and simmer for another 2 hours, checking for seasoning before serving.

Fish Tracker Salmon Chowder

3 tablespoons butter
1 cup onions, diced
2 cups celery, diced
4 large potatoes, peeled and diced
2 tablespoons cornstarch
1 cup evaporated milk
2 cups cooked salmon

In a soup pot, sauté the celery and onions in butter until tender and brown. Add the potatoes and water to cover. Simmer for about 30 minutes, or until the potatoes are tender. Stir the cornstarch into 1 cup of water and add to the mixture. Simmer until the mixture has thickened. Add the milk and salmon. Serve hot after checking for seasoning.

Off the Hook Chowder

$^1/_2$ pound smoked bacon, diced

I teaspoon paprika

$^2/_3$ cup onions, diced

I cup potatoes, diced

$^1/_2$ cup canned clams, chopped with juice

$^1/_4$ cup white wine

I cup cooked crabmeat, chopped

I cup shrimp, peeled

I cup scallops, halved and quartered

I teaspoon sea salt

Pepper to taste

I bay leaf

$^1/_2$ teaspoon thyme

3 cups milk

$^1/_3$ cup instant mashed potatoes (to thicken)

In a large soup kettle, brown the bacon with the paprika, onions, and potatoes until the potatoes are soft and the bacon is fully cooked. Add the clams, wine, crabmeat, shrimp, and scallops. Season with salt and pepper to taste, and add the bay leaf and thyme. Stir in the milk and simmer on low heat, stirring constantly. When the meat is thoroughly heated through, thicken the chowder by adding the instant mashed potatoes. Remove the bay leaf and serve.

Whopper Stopper Crab Vittles

$^1/_4$ cup butter

I pound crabmeat, flaked

I cup heavy whipping cream

$^1/_4$ cup Scotch whiskey

I quart milk

Salt and white pepper to taste

Chopped parsley to garnish

Melt the butter in a large soup pot. Stir in the crabmeat, cream, and Scotch. Simmer on low heat for about 5 minutes. Stir in the milk and season with salt and pepper. Simmer on very low heat for about 15 minutes. Serve in warm bowls garnished with chopped parsley.

Worm Dangler Stew

6 tablespoons olive oil
I cup onions, chopped
2 garlic cloves, chopped
$^2/_3$ cup fresh parsley, chopped
I cup fresh tomato, chopped
I teaspoon tomato paste
8 ounces clam juice
$^2/_3$ cup dry white wine
2 pounds sea bass fillets, chopped
Dry oregano to taste
Tabasco sauce to taste
Thyme to taste
White pepper to taste

Heat the olive oil in Dutch oven over medium-high heat. Add the chopped onions and garlic, and sauté until tender. Add the parsley and stir well for about 2 minutes. Add the tomato and tomato paste, and stir for another 2 to 3 minutes longer. Add the clam juice, dry white wine, and chopped fish fillets, and simmer until the fish is cooked through. Add the seasonings to taste and serve in warm bowls.

Cousin Rick's Crawfish and Corn Chowder

4 tablespoons butter

I large onion, diced

$^1/_2$ cup celery, diced

2 cloves garlic, diced

4 tablespoons flour

4 cups corn

4 cups chicken stock

I bunch green onions, chopped fine

$^1/_4$ cup parsley, chopped

2 tablespoons Frank's Red Hot Sauce

I pound crawfish tails, cooked

2 cups heavy cream

In a soup pot, sauté the onions and celery in butter over medium heat until tender and soft. Whisk in the garlic and flour, stirring until well blended. Add the corn and chicken stock, stirring until the soup begins to thicken and bubble. Add the green onions, parsley, and Frank's Red Hot Sauce. Simmer for about 25 minutes longer. Add the crawfish and cream. Simmer on low for about 5 minutes. Check the chowder for seasoning and serve hot in warm soup bowls.

Huston's Naut-a-Byte Seafood Gumbo

$^3/_4$ cup vegetable oil, divided

2 pounds fresh okra, thinly sliced

I tablespoon white vinegar

4 quarts chicken stock

2 pounds cooked ham, cubed

3 large onions, diced

2 stalks celery, chopped

I head garlic, cloves peeled but left whole

I green bell pepper, diced

I cup canned tomatoes, drained and chopped

4 pounds shrimp, shelled and deveined

2 pounds lump crabmeat

2 tablespoons Louisiana hot sauce

6 cups cooked long-grain rice

Heat $1/2$ cup oil in a large nonstick skillet over medium heat and add the okra slices. Simmer, stirring often, for about 35 minutes. Add the vinegar and cook, stirring, for about 15 more minutes, until the okra begins to brown. Place the cooked okra in a bowl and set aside. In a large soup pot over high heat, bring the stock to a boil. Meanwhile, add the remaining $1/4$ cup of oil and ham to the skillet. Sauté the ham until lightly browned. Remove the ham to the soup pot. In the same skillet, combine the onions, celery, garlic, and green pepper and cook, stirring constantly, until the vegetables are soft and tender. Add the cooked vegetables, cooked okra, and tomatoes to the soup pot; cover and simmer on low heat for about 15 minutes. Add the shrimp, crabmeat, and hot sauce; simmer for another 10 minutes. Serve the gumbo in soup bowls over a mound of cooked rice.

Braggin' Rights Tasty Clam Soup

I large onion, chopped

2 ribs celery, diced

2 carrots, diced

I garlic clove, minced

2 tablespoons olive oil

2 cups canned tomatoes, chopped

6 cups bottled clam juice

Red pepper flakes to taste

3 pounds smoked Polish sausage, chopped in thin rounds

2 cups chopped clams, cooked

$1/3$ cup fresh parsley, minced

In a large cast-iron skillet, sauté the onions, celery, carrots, and garlic in oil over low heat, stirring, until the vegetables are soft and tender. Stir in the tomatoes, clam juice, and red pepper flakes to taste. Simmer the mixture, covered, for about 5 minutes. In a heavy skillet, brown the sausage and drain on paper towels. Add the cooked clams and sausage to the tomato mixture and simmer for about 15 minutes. Stir in the parsley and check the soup for seasoning. Serve hot in warm soup bowls.

Fin-Addict Fish Stock

I pound fish bones, rinsed and cut into chunks
I small onion, peeled and quartered
I leek, white part only, peeled and quartered
I celery rib with leaves, sliced
10 shallots, sliced
2 large garlic cloves, sliced
I quart water
4 sprigs fresh flat-leaf parsley
2 fresh thyme sprigs
2 fresh tarragon sprigs
Zest of I lemon
I teaspoon fennel seeds
5 black peppercorns
I cup dry white wine

Combine the fish bones, onion, leeks, celery, shallots, garlic, and water in a large stockpot or a heavy saucepan. Bring to a boil over medium heat. Skim off any foam that rises to the top. Add the parsley, thyme, tarragon, lemon zest, fennel seeds, and peppercorns. Cover, reduce the heat, and simmer for about 20 minutes. Add the wine and simmer for about 15 minutes more. Strain through a fine sieve or a colander with cheesecloth. Discard the solids. Store in a sealed container in the refrigerator for up to 24 hours, or freeze for your next recipe calling for fish stock.

Y-Knot Tavern Oyster Mushroom Chowder

I quart oysters
I quart oyster liquor
3 tablespoons butter, sweet
I tablespoon flour
I cup milk
1/2 cup cream
3 tablespoons shallots, minced
2 teaspoons parsley
Salt and pepper to taste
1/2 pound mushrooms

Heat the oysters in liquor over low heat until the edges curl. Drain, saving the liquor. Melt 1 tablespoon butter and blend it with the flour; add the milk gradually, stirring constantly. Bring to a boil and then reduce to a low simmer. Add the cream, shallots, parsley, salt, and pepper to taste. Warm the mushrooms in the remaining butter until heated but not browned. Combine the cooked mushrooms, oysters, and oyster liquor to cream sauce. Stir and check again for seasonings. Serve immediately over Vista Bakery oyster crackers.

CHIP OFF THE OLD STUMP!

Cousin Rick took his son Travis fishing on his sixteenth birthday. As they were fishing, Cousin Rick pulled out a bottle of whiskey and took a drink. Travis was feeling his oats, so he asked dad if he could have a drink. Cousin Rick took two glasses out and filled one with water and the other with whiskey. He then pulled a worm out of a container and dropped it into the water glass. The worm wiggled around and looked very happy in the water. Cousin Rick then dropped a second worm into the glass of whiskey and the worm dropped to the bottom of the glass and died a horrible death. Cousin Rick then asked Travis what lesson he learned from the demonstration. Travis being a smart-tongued devil like his old man replied, "I should drink whiskey so I won't get worms."

Holland Grill Grilled Seafood Soup

This is not only fun to cook, but tastes great on my Holland Grill.

Medium potato
I medium onion, cubed
3 ounces Portuguese sausage
I hot cherry pepper
2 cups water
2 cups brown ale
12 clams
12 scallops
12 shrimp
12 mussels
Brad Holland seasoning salt to taste
Black pepper to taste
I tablespoon red bell pepper
I tablespoon parsley
Broth

Place the potato, onion, sausage, cherry pepper, water, and beer in a soup pan. Simmer until the potato is tender. Add the clams, cover, and cook until the clams open. Remove from heat, remove the clams, strain the broth, and hold. Grill the scallops and shrimp on Holland Grill with the lid closed until both are just cooked. Add water to the Holland Grill drip pan, close the drip valve, and steam the mussels until they open. Finely dice the red bell pepper and snip the parsley. Arrange the scallops, shrimp, mussels, and clams in a bowl; add seasoned salt and pepper and garnish. Pour hot broth over at the tableside and tear 'em up.

Hartschuh's Lake Catfish Soup

2 tablespoons butter
I large onion, chopped
3 pounds catfish, cut up
2 quarts cold water
I stalk celery, chopped
I cup milk
I bay leaf
I tablespoon parsley
I teaspoon thyme
Seasoning salt and pepper to taste

Melt the butter in the bottom of a large soup pan. Add the chopped onions and sauté until tender. Add the remaining ingredients and simmer over medium low heat until the catfish is almost ready to fall apart, about 3 hours. Check the soup for seasoning and serve hot.

Fins Up! Seafood Soup

1 onion, sliced thin
1 cup green onions with tops, chopped
3 cloves garlic, chopped fine
$^1/_2$ cup parsley, chopped fine
1 green bell pepper, diced
3 cups tomato sauce
1 cup dry white wine
1 cup water
$^1/_2$ teaspoon crushed thyme
$^1/_2$ teaspoon crushed rosemary
1 teaspoon salt
Pepper to taste
1 bay leaf
1 pound white fish, cubed
1 pound shrimp
6 scallops or clams in the shell

Combine the onions and garlic and cook, covered, over low heat until tender, stirring frequently so they don't scorch. Add the parsley, bell pepper, tomato sauce, wine, water, thyme, rosemary, salt, pepper, and bay leaf. Simmer covered, for about 60 minutes. Add the white fish, shrimp, scallops or clams, and cook, covered, for about 10 minutes, or until the clam shells open. Discard any shells that do not open. Serve soup hot after checking for seasoning.

Avid Angler Cod Stew

$^1/_4$ cup butter
5 carrots, peeled and sliced
2 yellow onions, chopped
2 pounds red potatoes, peeled and sliced
5 tomatoes, chopped
Salt and pepper to taste
Water
2 tablespoons flour
$^1/_2$ cup whole milk
3 fillets of cod
Dill
Parsley

Melt the butter in a large saucepan. Add the carrots and onions and cook until soft. Add the potatoes in layers and then layer the tomatoes over the potatoes. Season well with salt and pepper. Add enough water to come underneath top layer. Boil slowly for about 25 minutes. Mix the flour and milk for a thickener and add to the stew. Lay the cod fillets on top of stew and simmer for about 25 minutes. Sprinkle the dill and parsley over the top of the stew. This stew is outstanding served over hot cooked long-grain rice.

Reel Crazy Creole Fish Soup

I pound red snapper, deboned and shredded
I cup minced onions
I cup cooked strained tomatoes
I large bay leaf
Cayenne pepper to taste
I pound shelled shrimp, diced
I cup diced potatoes
I tablespoon butter
Creole seasoning
Salt and white pepper to taste
6 cups chicken stock
2 tablespoon fresh lemon juice

Combine all the ingredients, except the lemon juice, in a large saucepan or soup kettle. Simmer for about 45 minutes, or until the vegetables are tender. Add the lemon juice, check the soup for seasoning, and serve hot in warm soup bowls.

Rusty Reel Soup of the Sea

2 cups onions, chopped
2 cloves garlic, chopped
I cup green bell pepper, chopped
I cup celery, chopped
$^1/_4$ cup olive oil
I 14-ounce can tomatoes
I 16-ounce can tomato sauce
I teaspoon thyme
I teaspoon basil
I teaspoon oregano
Salt and pepper to taste
I cup dry red wine
I cup clam juice
$^1/_4$ pound shrimp, peeled and halved
I pound grouper fillets, cubed
$^1/_2$ pound crab pieces
$^1/_2$ pound small scallops
Fresh parsley for garnish

In a Dutch oven, sauté the onions, garlic, green pepper, and celery in oil until soft but not brown. Add the tomatoes, tomato sauce, herbs and spices, wine, and clam juice. Heat to boiling, and then simmer for about 45 minutes. Add the shrimp, fish, crab, and scallops to soup. Simmer for another 15 minutes. Add more clam juice if needed. Serve in warm soup bowls garnished with fresh parsley.

Anglers Edge Clear Fish Soup

4 cups chicken stock
$1/2$ pound trout fillets
I bunch fresh spinach
8 slices winter bamboo shoots
I teaspoon sea salt
I tablespoon cooking sherry
I tablespoon peanut oil

In a soup pot, heat the chicken stock. Cut the fillets into 1-inch pieces. Cut off the root ends of the spinach and thoroughly wash. Slice the bamboo shoots into very thin strips and add to the stock as it is simmering. Using a wire strainer, blanch the fish pieces in boiling water for about 20 seconds, and reserve. Add salt to the water and blanch the spinach for about 20 seconds; drain and reserve. When the stock reaches a rapid simmer, add the fish, spinach, and sherry. Simmer for about 5 minutes. Heat the peanut oil in a ladle over flame and mix into soup. Check the soup for seasoning and serve hot in warm bowls.

Cod Squad Fish Soup

2 tablespoons olive oil
I cup celery, sliced
I large white onion, sliced
2 large garlic cloves, sliced thin
2 pounds codfish bones and head
I quart chicken stock
I0 black peppercorns
I teaspoon dried thyme, crumbled
I teaspoon sea salt
¹/₂ teaspoon fennel seeds
2 pounds cod, cut in chunks
I¹/₂ cups grapefruit juice
I cup bottled clam juice

Heat the olive oil in a large, heavy pot and sauté the celery, onions, and garlic until tender. Add fish bones and head, chicken stock, peppercorns, thyme, sea salt, and fennel seeds. Bring to a boil, cover, reduce the heat, and simmer for about 45 minutes. Skim off any foam that rises to the surface. Strain the soup, discard flavorings, and return the soup to the pot. Add the fish, grapefruit juice, and clam juice. Simmer the soup for another 20 minutes on low heat. Check the soup for seasoning and serve hot.

SAD BUT TRUE!

Four married buddies go fishing. After an hour, the following conversation took place. First buddy: "You have no idea what I had to do to be able to come out fishing this weekend. I had to promise my wife that I will paint every room in the house next weekend." Second buddy: "That's nothing. I had to promise my wife that I would build her a new deck for the pool." Third buddy: "Man, you both have it easy! I had to promise my wife that I will remodel the kitchen for her." They continued to fish when they realized that Cousin Rick had not said a word. So they asked him: "Hey Cousin Rick, you haven't said anything about what you had to do to be able to come fishing this weekend. What's the deal?" Cousin Rick said, "Well boys,

I just set my alarm for 4:30 A.M. When it went off, I shut off my alarm, gave Becky a nudge and said, "Fishing or whoopee," and she said, "Wear a sweater!"

Castaway Tomato and Lobster Soup

2 ounces olive oil
I large white onion, finely diced
I serrano chile, diced
2 tomatillos, sliced
5 large, ripe yellow tomatoes
2 cups lobster stock
$^1/_2$ teaspoon salt
$^1/_2$ teaspoon white pepper
$^1/_2$ teaspoon cumin
2 cups cooked lobster meat, chopped

In a saucepan, sauté the onions in oil until tender but not browned. Add the chile and tomatillos and simmer over low heat until tender. Add the tomatoes and lobster stock. Simmer on low heat for about 25 minutes. Puree and season to taste with salt, white pepper, and cumin. Chill thoroughly and serve over cooked lobster meat in chilled bowls.

Island Lure Seafood Soup

3 cups chicken stock
$1/2$ cup frozen sweet corn kernels
$1/4$ teaspoon crushed red pepper flakes
$1/4$ cup tarragon vinegar
1 tablespoon freshly squeezed lime juice
2 tablespoons fresh parsley, chopped
$1/4$ teaspoon ground white pepper
1 teaspoon Accent
$1/4$ teaspoon garlic powder
1 pound small shrimp, peeled
$1/2$ cup calico scallops

In a heavy soup pot, bring the chicken stock to a low boil. Add the remaining ingredients and simmer for about 10 minutes. Check this soup for seasoning; adjust the tarragon vinegar to taste if needed.

Trout Time Stew

2 pounds trout fillets, cut in soup-sized cubes
2 tablespoons melted butter
1 clove garlic, minced
1 large onion, sliced
1 green bell pepper, chopped
2 zucchini squash, sliced
1 15-ounce can tomatoes, whole
$1/2$ teaspoon basil
$1/2$ teaspoon oregano
1 teaspoon garlic salt
$1/4$ teaspoon white pepper
$1/4$ cup dry white wine
$3/4$ cup fresh mushrooms

Combine all the ingredients in a large slow cooker. Stir gently but thoroughly. Cover and cook on high for about 6 hours. Stir the stew often and add chicken stock if needed. Serve the stew in warm soup bowls over cooked wild rice or noodles.

Still Jerkin' Crappie Chowder

$^1/_2$ cup chopped white onion
I tablespoon butter
2 cups milk
I cup ranch salad dressing
I pound crappie fillets
2 cups frozen broccoli, thawed
I cup shredded cheddar cheese
I cup shredded Monterey jack cheese
$^1/_2$ teaspoon garlic powder
Paprika to taste

In a large skillet, sauté the onion in butter until tender but not browned. Transfer to slow cooker; add milk, salad dressing, fillets, broccoli, both cheeses, and garlic powder. Cover and cook on high setting for about 2 hours, or until the soup is bubbly and the crappie meat flakes easily with a fork. Sprinkle the top of the soup with paprika to taste.

Jesse Johnson's "Fishy Business" Stew

Old Jesse is one of them edge-u-kate-d hillbillies that love his stew!

6 strips of heavy smoked bacon, chopped
I large yellow onion, chopped
3 large baking potatoes, diced
I 28-ounce can Italian-style tomatoes
I cup very dry vermouth
I tablespoon Worcestershire sauce
4 bay leaves
3 cloves garlic, minced
White pepper to taste
2 pounds catfish fillets, cubed into stew-sized chunks
Seasoning salt to taste

In a small Dutch oven, cook the bacon over medium heat until crisp. Add the onions and potatoes; cook, stirring, until the onion is tender, about 10 minutes. Add the tomatoes after breaking them up with a wooden spoon; include the tomato juice from the can. Stir in the vermouth, Worcestershire sauce, bay leaves, garlic, and white pepper to taste. Cover and simmer from about 30 minutes, or until the potatoes are good and tender. Add the remaining ingredients and simmer, covered, for about 30 more minutes, stirring every 15 minutes and checking for seasoning.

Cousin Rick's "Hook, Line, and Sinker" Stew

2 teaspoons butter
2 stalks celery, chopped
$^1/_2$ cup finely chopped white onions
4 cups chicken stock
I bay leaf
$^1/_4$ teaspoon sea salt
Pepper to taste
8 small red potatoes, quartered
2 pounds walleye fillets
$^1/_2$ pound bay scallops
I teaspoon minced fresh thyme
2 tablespoons minced fresh parsley

Melt the butter in a large saucepan over medium heat. Add the celery and onion and sauté until the onion is tender but not browned. Add the chicken stock, bay leaf, and salt. Pepper to taste. Bring to a boil over high heat, reduce the heat to low, and simmer for about 15 minutes. Raise the heat to medium, add the potatoes, and cook until nearly fork tender, about 15 minutes. Cut the walleye fillets into 1-inch pieces and add to the pan along with the scallops. Cook until just opaque. Add the thyme and parsley. Taste the stew for seasoning and serve hot in warm bowls.

Grouper Dodger Stew

3 pounds grouper fillets
Dark rum for soaking
Salt and lemon pepper
2 tablespoons oil
2 large yellow onions, sliced
3 scallions, chopped
3 large garlic cloves, minced
I large green bell pepper, chopped
3 large tomatoes, chopped
Scotch Bonnet pepper to taste
Fresh thyme to taste
$^1/_2$ teaspoon ground allspice
2 cups Miller Lite Beer
Salt and pepper to taste
$^1/_2$ teaspoon Kitchen Bouquet browning sauce
I tablespoon lime juice

Soak the fillets for about 5 minutes in dark rum. Pat the fillets dry and marinate with salt and lemon pepper in the cooler for about 4 hours. Heat 2 tablespoons oil in a large skillet over medium heat. Add the fillets to the skillet and brown on both sides. Remove the fish and carefully pour off the excess oil. Return the skillet to the stovetop. Cook the onions, scallions, garlic, green pepper, tomatoes, Scotch Bonnet, and thyme. Add the remaining ingredients and stir. Raise the heat to high and bring the stew to a boil. Reduce the heat and add the fillets. Simmer until sauce has thickened. Check the stew for seasoning and serve hot in warm stew bowls. This stew is very good with oyster crackers.

COUSIN RICK, NATURE'S BEST FRIEND!

Cousin Rick went fishing one day. He looked over the side of his boat and saw a snake with a frog in its mouth. Feeling sorry for the frog, he reached down, gently took the frog from the snake, and set the frog free. But then he felt sorry for the snake. He looked around the boat, but he had no food. All he had was a bottle of bourbon. So old Cousin Rick opened the bottle and gave the snake a few shots.

The snake went off happy, the frog was happy, and Cousin Rick felt very good about his deed. He thought everything was great until about ten minutes passed and he heard something knock against the side of the boat. With stunned disbelief, Cousin Rick looked down and saw the snake was back with two frogs!

Iowa on the Ocean Seafood and Corn Soup

16 ounces cooked Iowa corn
1 tablespoon cornstarch
$^{1}/_{4}$ cup water
4 cups chicken stock
1 teaspoon ginger root
$^{3}/_{4}$ pound fresh crabmeat
1 cup green onions, minced
Sea salt to taste
Pepper to taste
Rice vinegar to taste

In a large blender, add about half of the corn. Process until the corn is finely chopped. Add the remaining corn. Stir well and set aside. Combine the cornstarch and water in a small mixing bowl; stir well and set aside. Combine the chicken stock and ginger root in a large heavy saucepan; bring to a boil, add the corn, cornstarch mixture, crabmeat, green onions, salt, pepper, and vinegar to taste. Bring the soup to a boil. Reduce the heat to a simmer and simmer for about 20 minutes, stirring often. Check the soup again for seasoning and serve hot in warm soup bowls. This soup is very good served over noodles.

Pool Setter's Cream Of Crab Soup

2 chicken bouillon cubes
2 cups boiling water
$^1/_2$ cup chopped green onions
I cup sweet butter
5 tablespoons flour
$^1/_2$ teaspoon celery salt
$^1/_2$ teaspoon fresh-ground white pepper
I quart whole milk
2 pounds crabmeat
$^1/_4$ cup chopped parsley

Dissolve the bouillon cubes in the water. In a heavy stockpot, sauté the onions in butter until tender but not browned. Blend in the flour and seasoning to taste. Add the milk and bouillon broth slowly to the pot. Cook on low heat until the broth starts to thicken, stirring constantly. Add the remaining ingredients and simmer on low for about 20 more minutes. Check the soup for seasoning and serve hot.

Kenny's Fishin' Sea Oyster and Artichoke Soup

A Cousin Rick favorite!

2 cups artichoke hearts
4 tablespoons butter
4 tablespoons flour
I dozen fresh oysters
I cup whole milk
6 green onions, chopped
I large clove garlic, minced
I teaspoon dried thyme
¹/₄ cup chopped parsley
Sea salt and white pepper to taste
I cup heavy cream
I teaspoon Accent

Reserve ¹/₂ cup of the artichoke hearts for garnish; cut each into four pieces and set aside. Place the remaining 1¹/₂ cups in a food blender and blend well. Make a roux with the butter and flour, letting them cook together, stirring, but not browning. Stir in the artichoke puree, any liquid from the oysters, and milk. Simmer with the green onions, garlic, thyme, parsley, and salt and pepper for about 20 minutes in a large saucepan. Add the oysters and cream and simmer just until the oysters plump and curl around the edges. Add the Accent and serve hot in warm bowls topped with reserved artichokes.

Wishn'-Fishn' Shrimp Chowder

3 tablespoons salad oil

2 cups onion, diced

2 cloves garlic, diced

3 large tomatoes, chopped

3 red potatoes, cubed

I teaspoon ground chile pepper

^{1}/$_2$ teaspoon seasoned salt

I teaspoon sea salt

I teaspoon Accent

I teaspoon red pepper flakes

^{1}/$_4$ teaspoon Frank's Red Hot Sauce

2 cups whole milk

4 grouper fillets

^{1}/$_2$ cup cream cheese

^{2}/$_3$ pounds shrimp, shelled and deveined

2 cups canned sweet corn

2 sprigs mint

In a large soup pot, sauté the onions and garlic in oil until tender. Add the tomatoes, potatoes, chile pepper, salts, Accent, red pepper flakes, Frank's Red Hot Sauce, milk, and about 4 cups water; stir occasionally, while bringing to a low boil. Reduce the heat and simmer, covered, for about 30 minutes. Meanwhile, in 1 cup water and $\frac{1}{2}$ teaspoon sea salt in a skillet, simmer the fish fillets for about 8 minutes, or until fork tender but still moist. In a mixing bowl, beat the cream cheese with about $\frac{1}{4}$ cup milk until smooth. Stir the cream cheese mixture, shrimp, and sweet corn into the soup, and cook over medium heat for about 6 minutes. Drain the fillets and place them into soup bowls. Spoon hot soup mixture over the fillets in bowls and garnish with sprigs of mint.

High Hook Bluefish Chowder

6 slices thick-cut smoked bacon, chopped

I cup diced white onions

I pound bluefish fillets, cut in soup-sized cubes

I cup celery, chopped

2 cups diced red potatoes

3 cups chicken stock

I teaspoon seasoned salt

$^1/_2$ teaspoon sea salt

I teaspoon dried tarragon

$^1/_2$ teaspoon rosemary

$^1/_2$ tablespoon parsley, diced

$^1/_2$ teaspoon white pepper

$^1/_2$ teaspoon dried basil

4 tablespoons butter

4 tablespoons flour

13 ounces evaporated milk

Crisp the bacon in a large saucepan over medium heat; add the onions and sauté until tender. Add the bluefish and cook, stirring occasionally, until the meat begins to brown. Add the remaining ingredients, except the butter, flour, and evaporated milk, and simmer until the potatoes are tender. Melt the butter in a heavy saucepan over low heat; add the flour, stirring until smooth. Cook for about 1 minute, stirring constantly. Gradually add the milk; cook over medium heat, stirring constantly, until thick and bubbly. Stir this sauce into the fish mixture; simmer, stirring occasionally, for about 30 minutes, or until the chowder is thick. Check the chowder for seasoning and serve hot.

Nautifish Flounder Soup

3 pounds flounder fillets
2 cups diced white onions
1 crushed garlic clove
4 tablespoons butter
8 red potatoes, peeled and quartered
10 cups strong chicken stock
2 bay leaves
1 teaspoon thyme
$^1/_2$ teaspoon marjoram
4 sprigs parsley
2 teaspoons sea salt
Fresh-ground white pepper to taste

Cut the fillets into stew-sized cubes. Sauté the onions and garlic in butter in a large soup pot until all are tender. Add the red potatoes, stock, bay leaves, thyme, marjoram, parsley, sea salt, and white pepper to taste. Bring to a boil. Add the fish cubes and lower the heat to a simmer. Cook, covered, for about 35 minutes, or until the potatoes are good and tender. Remove the bay leaves. Check the soup for seasoning and serve hot. This soup is great over toasted garlic bread.

Bait Master Soup

2 lime leaves
Juice of a lemon
2 cups fish stock
$^1/_2$ teaspoon ginger
3 tablespoons fish sauce
$^1/_2$ pound shrimp
$^1/_4$ pound oysters
$^1/_4$ pound crabmeat
$^1/_2$ pound salmon fillets
$^1/_4$ pound scallops
1 cup coconut milk
Crushed red chile peppers to taste

In a heavy soup pot or soup kettle, chop the lime leaves and add the lemon juice, stock, ginger, and fish sauce. Bring to a boil, stirring well. Add the remaining ingredients and simmer on low heat for about 30 minutes, or until the seafood is tender. Serve hot over cooked rice.

Jaws' Revenge Shark Fin Soup

$1/2$ **pound dried shark's fin**
I cup white chicken meat
Cornstarch for coating
$1/2$ **cup smoked ham**
2 scallion stalks
6 cups chicken stock
I teaspoon cooking sherry
Sea salt to taste

Soak and process the shark's fin. Shred the chicken; then dredge the chicken lightly in the cornstarch. Dice the ham and scallion stalks. In a heavy soup pot, bring the stock to a boil. Add the shark's fin and simmer, covered, for about 30 minutes. Add the remaining ingredients and simmer for another 20 minutes.

COUSIN RICK'S TEN CLUES THAT YOU'VE MOST LIKELY CHOSEN THE WRONG FISHING GUIDE!

1. He's got the open engine manual sitting on the console next to the controls.
2. He screams "Yeehaa" as he turns the boat away from the dock and pushes the throttle forward.
3. He thinks it's an asset that he can drive so fast that he gets the boat completely out of the water.
4. It takes him two hours and twenty-five minutes to reach your fishing destination on a five-hour charter!
5. He can't stop laughing when he realizes that his brother the sheriff gave you a speeding ticket on your way to his boat, and says nothing about getting the ticket canceled.

6. He casually tells you that on days he can't get a charter he's a delivery driver for Bubba's Pizza Shack.

7. He goes on for hours about how boats are safer than cars, but only because there are fewer vehicles directly next to one to hit. He runs aground three times during this oration.

8. He goes on for hours about his alien abduction experiences, giving much detail on the tests they supposedly performed on him.

9. The other fishing guides hold up protective religious icons as he passes by.

10. At the end of the day's catchless fishing, he begs you to allow him to use your name as a reference, because none of his other 110 charters would!

CHAPTER SIX

COUSIN RICK'S FAVORITE CHILI, SOUP, AND STEW SIDES

This chapter has my favorite recipes that go great with your chilies, soups, and stews. This truly is a great tool for your home and cabin! Heck, if you're lucky, you might get your better half to cook these for ya while you're workin' on the soup!

Thousands of years ago in Europe, there was a reigning king that was a very avid hunter. In fact he was such an avid hunter that he passed a law banning all his subjects from hunting anywhere in his kingdom so he would have more game for himself! His subjects were outraged by the law as many of them were hunters as well. They became so enraged over their game hog leader that they overthrew the king, ending his reign. This Cousin Rick fans mark as the only time in history that a reign was called off, because of game!

I know, let's move on. . . .

Cabin Crackers

2 cups flour
1 teaspoon salt
$^1/_2$ teaspoon baking powder
$^1/_4$ cup butter
$^1/_2$ cup milk
1 large egg

Sift the flour, salt, and baking powder into a mixing bowl. Cut in the butter until very fine. Add the milk and egg and mix to make a stiff dough. Knead thoroughly and then roll the dough very thin. Cut into squares or rounds and place on lightly buttered cookie sheets. Prick the crackers with a fork and then bake in a 400-degree oven for about 10 minutes, or until very lightly browned. Top with coarse salt if desired.

Hog Wrasslin' Soda Crackers

4 cups flour
1 teaspoon baking powder
$^3/_4$ cup shortening
1$^1/_3$ cup milk

Mix the flour, baking powder, and shortening as for a piecrust. Add the milk and cut in with a knife. Form a ball of dough and cut into four pieces. Roll each quarter out very thin. Cut with a biscuit or cookie cutter and place on a cookie sheet. Prick with a fork and sprinkle with coarse or seasoned salt to your taste. Bake at 375 degrees until golden brown. Turn once if desired for even color.

Cleon's Cheddar Crackers

1 1/2 cups unbleached flour, sifted
1/2 teaspoon salt
1 teaspoon baking powder
1/4 teaspoon cayenne pepper
1/2 cup butter
2 cups extra sharp cheddar cheese, finely grated

Stir the dry ingredients into a mixing bowl and then cut in the butter until the mixture resembles cornmeal. Blend in the cheddar cheese with a fork until all is well mixed. Shape into 2-inch rolls. Chill for about 60 minutes in the refrigerator and then slice each roll into slices about 1/4-inch thick. Bake on an ungreased cookie sheet at 400 degrees for about 10 minutes. Remove from the cookie sheet and let cool. Top with coarse salt if desired.

Flannel Shirt Wheat Crackers

1/2 cup whole wheat flour
2 tablespoons butter
2 tablespoons sunflower seeds
1/8 teaspoon seasoned salt
1/2 cup cottage cheese

Place all the ingredients except the cottage cheese in a food processor and blend into fine crumbs. Transfer to a small mixing bowl. Add the cottage cheese to the food processor and blend until smooth. Add the flour mixture to the cottage cheese mixture and mix until it forms a ball shape. Roll out the dough ball thinly. Prick all areas of the dough with a fork. Cut crosswise into 4 equal strips and then lengthwise into 3 equal strips; next cut equally into fourths, to make about 48 cracker shapes. Bake the crackers at 325 degrees for about 20 minutes. Top with coarse salt if desired.

Great Value Hunter Vegetable Juice Crackers

2 cups flour
$^1/_2$ teaspoon salt
$^1/_2$ teaspoon cracked pepper
2 tablespoons butter, softened
$^2/_3$ cup, plus 1 tablespoon, Great Value vegetable juice
$^1/_4$ teaspoon Tabasco sauce

Preheat the oven to 325 degrees. Stir together the flour, salt, and pepper in a large mixing bowl. Cut in the butter until the mixture resembles coarse meal. In a separate bowl, mix the vegetable juice and hot sauce. Add the vegetable juice mixture to the flour mixture and blend to form a dough that will hold together in a cohesive ball. Divide into 2 equal portions for rolling. On a floured surface or pastry cloth, roll thin, about $^1/_8$-inch thick. With a sharp knife, cut the dough into 2-inch squares and place them on an ungreased baking sheet. Prick each square about 3 times with a fork. Bake for about 25 minutes, turning over after about 10 minutes. Top with salt if desired.

Juan's Jalapeño Cheese Crackers

$^1/_2$ cup sharp cheddar cheese, cubed
1 tablespoon jalapeño peppers, minced
$^1/_3$ cup cold butter, cubed
$^3/_4$ cup flour
$^1/_4$ cup cornmeal
$^1/_2$ teaspoon salt
$^1/_4$ teaspoon chili powder
$^1/_4$ teaspoon dry mustard
4 tablespoon ice water

Preheat the oven to 400 degrees. Process the cheese and jalapeño in a food processor until finely chopped. Add the butter, and pulse until blended well. Stir the flour with the cornmeal, salt, chili powder, and dry mustard in a mixing bowl until well blended. Add this to the mixture in the blender and blend together well. Add the ice water to the blender and pulse to form a dough. Shape the dough into an 8-inch disk. Wrap the dough disk in plastic wrap and refrigerate it until it becomes firm enough to roll, about 45 minutes. On a floured surface, roll the dough to $\frac{1}{4}$-inch thickness. Cut in 2-inch rounds with a cookie cutter or wine glass. Transfer to an ungreased baking sheet. Prick each cracker once with a fork. Bake in a preheated oven for about 12 minutes, or until crisp. Top with coarse salt if desired.

Cousin Rick's Dutch-Oven Taters

I pound thick-cut smoked bacon
2 cups onions, sliced
4 garlic cloves, diced
2 cups fresh mushrooms, sliced
16 red potatoes, peeled and sliced
I can cream of chicken soup
I can cheddar cheese soup
I cup sour cream
3 tablespoons Worcestershire sauce
I tablespoon soy sauce
I teaspoon parsley
Garlic salt and pepper to taste

Heat the Dutch oven using about 20 briquettes on the bottom until hot. Chop the bacon and fry in oven until crisp. Add the onions, garlic, and mushrooms. Cover and cook until the onions are tender. Add the red potato slices. Cook the potatoes until just brown. Add the remaining ingredients and cook for about 60 minutes using 15 briquettes on the bottom and about 12 on top. Check and stir the potatoes twice during the cooking process. Check the potatoes for seasoning before serving with your favorite wild game soup or stew.

HOW 'BOUT COOKIN' THAT STEW AT THE CAMPFIRE?

The campfire is the center of activity and gathering at our cabin. So it is a no-brainer that precautions need to be taken to make it a safe place. Cookin' over an open fire is most often the center of a camp outing, although there are some important things to keep in mind.

Speaking from years of experience, I can tell you that there are several items that create an ideal setup for your cooking. I always plan my cooking style ahead of time to accommodate my meal planning. Take your time so you don't sweat bullets when you're at the fire. Focus without distractions. Keep an eye on the kids so you need not worry or cook with little tikes at your heels. There are several outdoor pans and equipment that will work on fire and several others that are best left for home use or inside the camper or cabin. A Dutch oven with legs is a must! I have several Camp Chef ovens available when I am cooking for a large group of hungry hunters who want a ton of hot soup or stew.

I have found that the best cooking pot is cast iron with a lid that has a lip on it. This allows you to put hot coals on the top of it without sliding off. The coals on the top of the lid help the soup or stew cook from both the top and the bottom of the pan, kinda like the way your conventional oven works. This is the best way to cook at the fireside.

When it comes to pots and pans, I love cast iron. Use the longest utensils that are comfortable for you. The farther from the heat source you are, the safer you will be. Ain't nothin' worse than a burn on your trigger finger! Although they are heavier to transport, consider cast-iron utensils because of their durability. If cooking over a fire, avoid wood tools for obvious reasons. When cooking chilies, soups, and stews, a great selection is a spoon, a slotted spoon, and a long and shorter spatula.

Pick out a safe spot to set hot pans as they are coming off the fire (potholders, oven mitts, and dish towels are necessary). Be sure to also have an ash bucket, shovel, a bucket of water for emergencies, and a poker.

Wear appropriate clothing—nothing loose that will get in the way of your cookin' or catch on fire. Keep in mind that your soup or stew will likely burn if you put a pan atop hot coals. But your soup vittles can't cook if too far from the heat source. Always, when cooking is completed, be sure to cool all the coals or make sure that everyone is aware of them. I had a buddy once trash out a $200 pair of Rockies because of hot coals.

All in all, have fun!

Cooter's Sourdough Cornbread

2 cups sourdough starter
2¹/₄ cups canned milk
2¹/₄ cups yellow cornmeal
3 tablespoons sugar
3 eggs, beaten
8 tablespoons butter, melted
I teaspoon baking soda
I teaspoon Accent
Salt and pepper to taste

Mix the sourdough starter, milk, cornmeal, sugar, and eggs together and stir well. Add the melted butter, baking soda, Accent, salt, and pepper to taste. Add these ingredients together in a Dutch oven. Place the lid on the oven and bake using about 15 briquettes on the bottom and about 25 on top for about 30 minutes, or until the cornbread turns golden brown.

Cousin Rick's Stew Cake

4 cups sour milk

5 eggs, beaten

$^1/_4$ cup butter, soft

4 cups cornmeal

2 cups flour

2 cups wheat flour

$^1/_3$ cup sugar

2 teaspoons baking soda

I teaspoon baking powder

I teaspoon Accent

I teaspoon salt

In a large mixing bowl, blend together the milk, eggs, and soft butter. In another mixing bowl, sift together the cornmeal, flour, wheat flour, sugar, baking soda, baking powder, Accent, and salt. Mix the two ingredient bowls together and stir well. Spoon the cake batter into a greased Dutch oven and spread evenly. Place the cover on the oven and bake using 12 briquettes on the bottom and about 18 briquettes on top. Bake for about 60 minutes, or until the Cousin Rick cake is golden brown.

Six-Tooth Cletus Shotgun Cornbread Vittles

I cup butter, soft

4 eggs, beaten

3 cups milk

2 cups sugar

2 cups cornmeal

3 cups flour

4 teaspoons baking powder

I teaspoon garlic salt with parsley

$^1/_4$ teaspoon dry mustard

Mix together all the ingredients in a large mixing bowl until smooth. Lightly grease the Dutch oven and spread the mixture in it evenly. Cover and bake using about 12 briquettes on the bottom and about 18 on the top. Bake for about 50 minutes, or until the cornbread is golden brown. You can add about 1/4 teaspoon cayenne if you want "real Cletus Shotgun Cornmeal Vittles"!

Buford Biscuits

5 cups flour
2¹/₂ tablespoons baking powder
5 tablespoons sugar
3 teaspoons salt
I teaspoon white pepper
4 cups heavy cream, ice cold

Mix together all the ingredients in a large mixing bowl until they are smooth and form a solid dough. Use a biscuit cutter to form biscuits into shape. Place the biscuits in a lightly oiled Dutch oven leaving about 1/2-inch gap between each. Cover the Dutch oven and let the biscuits rise for about 15 minutes. Bake the biscuits using about 16 briquettes on the bottom and about 20 on the top. Bake for about 30 minutes, or until the biscuits are golden brown. Top the Buford biscuits with butter and serve with your favorite wild game soup, stew, or chili.

Beer-Chuggin', Mud-Diving Herb Rolls

1 1/2 cups warm water
1/2 cup dry milk
1/3 cup sugar
1 tablespoon quick dry yeast
2 eggs, beaten
5 cups flour
4 tablespoons dry minced onion
1 teaspoon dried dill weed
1 teaspoon dried rosemary
1 teaspoon dried thyme
3 tablespoons dried parsley
1 tablespoon garlic powder with parsley
1/3 cup corn oil
1 teaspoon salt
1 teaspoon pepper

In a large mixing bowl add the water, milk, sugar, and yeast. Stir well and let the mixture sit until it becomes bubbly. Add the eggs and about 3 cups flour, onion, dill weed, rosemary, thyme, and parsley. Blend together well. Let the mixture stand for about 10 minutes. Add the remaining ingredients and blend together until the dough becomes firm. Place the dough on a well-floured board and form into 2-inch balls. Place the dough balls in a well-oiled Dutch oven, cover, and let sit for about 15 minutes. Bake the Mud Divers until golden brown.

COUSIN RICK'S MEASURING TIPS

$\frac{1}{4}$ cup = 4 tablespoons

$\frac{1}{3}$ cup = 5 tablespoons plus 1 teaspoon

$\frac{1}{2}$ cup = 8 tablespoons

$\frac{2}{3}$ cup = 10 tablespoons plus 2 teaspoons

1 cup = 16 tablespoons

1 tablespoon = 3 teaspoons

2 tablespoons = 1 fluid ounce

1 cup = 8 fluid ounces

1 cup = $\frac{1}{2}$ pint

2 cups = 1 pint

4 cups = 1 quart

4 quarts = 1 gallon

RECOMMENDED SOURCES

This is my recommended list for hunters who don't fish and fishermen who don't hunt—some of the best outdoor cookery folks I know!

Pack Lite Foods, www.packlitefoods.com
Outstanding foods for camping, fishing, or trail hiking

Tink's, www.tinks69.com
Cousin Rick's choice for deer cover, buck lures, and outstanding scents. I successfully bagged wall-hangers with Tink's Draw 2 Deer Lure!

Camp Chef, www.campchef.com
Cousin Rick's choice in Dutch ovens and smokers. I really enjoy cooking with my Camp Chef ovens.

Snugpak, www.snugpackusa.com and www.proforceequipment.com
Outstanding outdoor gear, warm and handy. I always wear my Snugpak shirts and coats when the winter chill hits.

Holland Grill Company, www.hollandgrill.com
If you're lookin' you're not cookin', my choice in cookin'. I love my Holland Grill.

AdjustAGrill, www.adjustagrill.com
Grill on the go! The perfect grill for camp. Cousin Rick has cooked up many great-tastin' vittles on his AdustAGrill!

Campfire Grill, www.campfiregrill.com
I highly recommend the original. Jeff Walker and gang have mastered outdoor cookery. Deer burgers ain't ever tasted so good than cooked on my Campfire Original Grill!

Quarry Creek Elk & Bison Company, www.quarrycreek.com
Cousin Rick's choice when it comes to great-tastin' elk and buffalo. The pride of Fort Madison, Iowa!

Gamo Precision Airguns, www.gamousa.com
Outstanding weapons for target shooting and small-game hunting.

Baja Motorsports, www.bajamotorsports.net
Cousin Rick's choice in ATVs and outdoor transportation.

M2D Camo, www.m2dcamo.com
Cousin Rick's choice in all my hunting camo.

INDEX